ROMEO AND JULIET

William Shakespeare

SPARK PUBLISHING

Spark Publishing
A Division of Barnes & Noble
120 Fifth Avenue
New York, NY 10011
www.sparknotes.com

ISBN-13: 978-1-4114-0310-9
ISBN-10: 1-4114-0310-X

Please submit changes or report errors to www.sparknotes.com/errors.

Printed in the United States.

20 19 18 17 16 15 14 13 12 11

Contents

Context

THE MOST INFLUENTIAL WRITER IN ALL OF English literature, William Shakespeare was born in 1564 to a successful middle-class glove-maker in Stratford-upon-Avon, England. Shakespeare attended grammar school, but his formal education proceeded no further. In 1582 he married an older woman, Anne Hathaway, and had three children with her. Around 1590 he left his family behind and traveled to London to work as an actor and playwright. Public and critical success quickly followed, and Shakespeare eventually became the most popular playwright in England and part-owner of the Globe Theater. His career bridged the reigns of Elizabeth I (ruled 1558–1603) and James I (ruled 1603–1625), and he was a favorite of both monarchs. Indeed, James granted Shakespeare's company the greatest possible compliment by bestowing upon its members the title of King's Men. Wealthy and renowned, Shakespeare retired to Stratford and died in 1616 at the age of fifty-two. At the time of Shakespeare's death, literary luminaries such as Ben Jonson hailed his works as timeless.

Shakespeare's works were collected and printed in various editions in the century following his death, and by the early eighteenth century his reputation as the greatest poet ever to write in English was well established. The unprecedented admiration garnered by his works led to a fierce curiosity about Shakespeare's life, but the dearth of biographical information has left many details of Shakespeare's personal history shrouded in mystery. Some people have concluded from this fact that Shakespeare's plays were really written by someone else—Francis Bacon and the Earl of Oxford are the two most popular candidates—but the support for this claim is overwhelmingly circumstantial, and the theory is not taken seriously by many scholars.

In the absence of credible evidence to the contrary, Shakespeare must be viewed as the author of the thirty-seven plays and 154 sonnets that bear his name. The legacy of this body of work is immense. A number of Shakespeare's plays seem to have transcended even the category of brilliance, becoming so influential as to profoundly affect the course of Western literature and culture ever after.

Shakespeare did not invent the story of *Romeo and Juliet*. He did not, in fact, even introduce the story into the English language. A poet named Arthur Brooks first brought the story of *Romeus and Juliet* to an English-speaking audience in a long and plodding poem that was itself not original, but rather an adaptation of adaptations that stretched across nearly a hundred years and two languages. Many of the details of Shakespeare's plot are lifted directly from Brooks's poem, including the meeting of Romeo and Juliet at the ball, their secret marriage, Romeo's fight with Tybalt, the sleeping potion, and the timing of the lover's eventual suicides. Such appropriation of other stories is characteristic of Shakespeare, who often wrote plays based on earlier works.

Shakespeare's use of existing material as fodder for his plays should not, however, be taken as a lack of originality. Instead, readers should note how Shakespeare crafts his sources in new ways while displaying a remarkable understanding of the literary tradition in which he is working. Shakespeare's version of *Romeo and Juliet* is no exception. The play distinguishes itself from its predecessors in several important aspects: the subtlety and originality of its characterization (Shakespeare almost wholly created Mercutio); the intense pace of its action, which is compressed from nine months into four frenetic days; a powerful enrichment of the story's thematic aspects; and, above all, an extraordinary use of language.

Shakespeare's play not only bears a resemblance to the works on which it is based, it is also quite similar in plot, theme, and dramatic ending to the story of Pyramus and Thisbe, told by the great Roman poet Ovid in his *Metamorphoses*. Shakespeare was well aware of this similarity; he includes a reference to Thisbe in *Romeo and Juliet*. Shakespeare also includes scenes from the story of Pyramus and Thisbe in the comically awful play-within-a-play put on by Bottom and his friends in *A Midsummer Night's Dream*—a play Shakespeare wrote around the same time he was composing *Romeo and Juliet*. Indeed, one can look at the play-within-a-play in *A Midsummer Night's Dream* as parodying the very story that Shakespeare seeks to tell in *Romeo and Juliet*. Shakespeare wrote *Romeo and Juliet* in full knowledge that the story he was telling was old, clichéd, and an easy target for parody. In writing *Romeo and Juliet*, Shakespeare, then, implicitly set himself the task of telling a love story despite the considerable forces he knew were stacked against its success. Through the incomparable intensity of his language Shakespeare succeeded in this effort, writing a play that is universally accepted in Western culture as the preeminent, archetypal love story.

Plot Overview

In the streets of Verona another brawl breaks out between the servants of the feuding noble families of Capulet and Montague. Benvolio, a Montague, tries to stop the fighting, but is himself embroiled when the rash Capulet, Tybalt, arrives on the scene. After citizens outraged by the constant violence beat back the warring factions, Prince Escalus, the ruler of Verona, attempts to prevent any further conflicts between the families by decreeing death for any individual who disturbs the peace in the future.

Romeo, the son of Montague, runs into his cousin Benvolio, who had earlier seen Romeo moping in a grove of sycamores. After some prodding by Benvolio, Romeo confides that he is in love with Rosaline, a woman who does not return his affections. Benvolio counsels him to forget this woman and find another, more beautiful one, but Romeo remains despondent.

Meanwhile, Paris, a kinsman of the Prince, seeks Juliet's hand in marriage. Her father Capulet, though happy at the match, asks Paris to wait two years, since Juliet is not yet even fourteen. Capulet dispatches a servant with a list of people to invite to a masquerade and feast he traditionally holds. He invites Paris to the feast, hoping that Paris will begin to win Juliet's heart.

Romeo and Benvolio, still discussing Rosaline, encounter the Capulet servant bearing the list of invitations. Benvolio suggests that they attend, since that will allow Romeo to compare his beloved to other beautiful women of Verona. Romeo agrees to go with Benvolio to the feast, but only because Rosaline, whose name he reads on the list, will be there.

In Capulet's household, young Juliet talks with her mother, Lady Capulet, and her nurse about the possibility of marrying Paris. Juliet has not yet considered marriage, but agrees to look at Paris during the feast to see if she thinks she *could* fall in love with him.

The feast begins. A melancholy Romeo follows Benvolio and their witty friend Mercutio to Capulet's house. Once inside, Romeo sees Juliet from a distance and instantly falls in love with her; he forgets about Rosaline completely. As Romeo watches Juliet, entranced, a young Capulet, Tybalt, recognizes him, and is enraged that a Montague would sneak into a Capulet feast. He prepares to attack, but Capulet holds him back. Soon, Romeo speaks to Juliet, and the two experience a profound attraction. They kiss, not even knowing each other's names. When he finds out from Juliet's nurse that she is the daughter of Capulet—his family's enemy—he becomes distraught. When Juliet learns that the young man she has just kissed is the son of Montague, she grows equally upset.

As Mercutio and Benvolio leave the Capulet estate, Romeo leaps over the orchard wall into the garden, unable to leave Juliet behind. From his hiding place, he sees Juliet in a window above the orchard and hears her speak his name. He calls out to her, and they exchange vows of love.

Romeo hurries to see his friend and confessor Friar Lawrence, who, though shocked at the sudden turn of Romeo's heart, agrees to marry the young lovers in secret since he sees in their love the possibility of ending the age-old feud between Capulet and Montague. The following day, Romeo and Juliet meet at Friar Lawrence's cell and are married. The Nurse, who is privy to the secret, procures a ladder, which Romeo will use to climb into Juliet's window for their wedding night.

The next day, Benvolio and Mercutio encounter Tybalt—Juliet's cousin—who, still enraged that Romeo attended Capulet's feast, has challenged Romeo to a duel. Romeo appears. Now Tybalt's kinsman by marriage, Romeo begs the Capulet to hold off the duel until he understands why Romeo does not want to fight. Disgusted with this plea for peace, Mercutio says that he will fight Tybalt himself. The two begin to duel. Romeo tries to stop them by leaping between the combatants. Tybalt stabs Mercutio under Romeo's arm, and Mercutio dies. Romeo, in a rage, kills Tybalt. Romeo flees from the scene. Soon after, the Prince declares him forever banished from Verona for his crime. Friar Lawrence arranges for Romeo to spend his wedding night with Juliet before he has to leave for Mantua the following morning.

In her room, Juliet awaits the arrival of her new husband. The Nurse enters, and, after some confusion, tells Juliet that Romeo has killed Tybalt. Distraught, Juliet suddenly finds herself married to a man who has killed her kinsman. But she resettles herself, and realizes that her duty belongs with her love: to Romeo.

Romeo sneaks into Juliet's room that night, and at last they consummate their marriage and their love. Morning comes, and the lovers bid farewell, unsure when they will see each other again. Juliet learns that her father, affected by the recent events, now intends for her to marry Paris in just three days. Unsure of how to proceed—unable to reveal to her parents that she is married to Romeo, but unwilling to marry Paris now that she is Romeo's wife—Juliet asks her Nurse for advice. She counsels Juliet to proceed as if Romeo were dead and to marry Paris, who is a better match anyway. Disgusted with the Nurse's disloyalty, Juliet disregards her advice and hurries to Friar Lawrence. He concocts a plan to reunite Juliet with Romeo in Mantua. The night before her wedding to Paris, Juliet must drink a potion that will make her appear to be dead. After she is laid to rest in the family's crypt, the Friar and Romeo will secretly retrieve her, and she will be free to live with Romeo, away from their parents' feuding.

Juliet returns home to discover the wedding has been moved ahead one day, and she is to be married tomorrow. That night, Juliet drinks the potion, and the Nurse discovers her, apparently dead, the next morning. The Capulets grieve, and Juliet is entombed according to plan. But Friar Lawrence's message explaining the plan to Romeo never reaches Mantua. Its bearer, Friar John, gets confined to a quarantined house. Romeo hears only that Juliet is dead.

Romeo learns only of Juliet's death and decides to kill himself rather than live without her. He buys a vial of poison from a reluctant Apothecary, then speeds back to Verona to take his own life at Juliet's tomb. Outside the Capulet crypt, Romeo comes upon Paris, who is scattering flowers on Juliet's grave. They fight, and Romeo kills Paris. He enters the tomb, sees Juliet's inanimate body, drinks the poison, and dies by her side. Just then, Friar Lawrence enters and realizes that Romeo has killed Paris and himself. At the same time, Juliet awakes. Friar Lawrence hears the coming of the watch. When Juliet refuses to leave with him, he flees alone. Juliet sees her beloved Romeo and realizes he has killed himself with poison. She kisses his poisoned lips, and when that does not kill her, buries his dagger in her chest, falling dead upon his body.

The watch arrives, followed closely by the Prince, the Capulets, and Montague. Montague declares that Lady Montague has died of grief over Romeo's exile. Seeing their children's bodies, Capulet and Montague agree to end their long-standing feud and to raise gold statues of their children side-by-side in a newly peaceful Verona.

Character List

Romeo The son and heir of Montague and Lady Montague. A young man of about sixteen, Romeo is handsome, intelligent, and sensitive. Though impulsive and immature, his idealism and passion make him an extremely likable character. He lives in the middle of a violent feud between his family and the Capulets, but he is not at all interested in violence. His only interest is love. At the beginning of the play he is madly in love with a woman named Rosaline, but the instant he lays eyes on Juliet, he falls in love with her and forgets Rosaline. Thus, Shakespeare gives us every reason to question how real Romeo's new love is, but Romeo goes to extremes to prove the seriousness of his feelings. He secretly marries Juliet, the daughter of his father's worst enemy; he happily takes abuse from Tybalt; and he would rather die than live without his beloved. Romeo is also an affectionate and devoted friend to his relative Benvolio, Mercutio, and Friar Lawrence.

Juliet The daughter of Capulet and Lady Capulet. A beautiful thirteen-year-old girl, Juliet begins the play as a naïve child who has thought little about love and marriage, but she grows up quickly upon falling in love with Romeo, the son of her family's great enemy. Because she is a girl in an aristocratic family, she has none of the freedom Romeo has to roam around the city, climb over walls in the middle of the night, or get into swordfights. Nevertheless, she shows amazing courage in trusting her entire life and future to Romeo, even refusing to believe the worst reports about him after he gets involved in a fight with her cousin. Juliet's closest friend and confidant is her Nurse, though she's willing to shut the Nurse out of her life the moment the Nurse turns against Romeo.

Friar Lawrence A Franciscan friar, friend to both Romeo and Juliet. Kind, civic-minded, a proponent of moderation, and always ready with a plan, Friar Lawrence secretly marries the impassioned lovers in hopes that the union might eventually bring peace to Verona. As well as being a Catholic holy man, Friar Lawrence is also an expert in the use of seemingly mystical potions and herbs.

Mercutio A kinsman to the Prince, and Romeo's close friend. One of the most extraordinary characters in all of Shakespeare's plays, Mercutio overflows with imagination, wit, and, at times, a strange, biting satire and brooding fervor. Mercutio loves wordplay, especially sexual double entendres. He can be quite hotheaded, and hates people who are affected, pretentious, or obsessed with the latest fashions. He finds Romeo's romanticized ideas about love tiresome, and tries to convince Romeo to view love as a simple matter of sexual appetite.

The Nurse Juliet's nurse, the woman who breast-fed Juliet when she was a baby and has cared for Juliet her entire life. A vulgar, long-winded, and sentimental character, the Nurse provides comic relief with her frequently inappropriate remarks and speeches. But, until a disagreement near the play's end, the Nurse is Juliet's faithful confidante and loyal intermediary in Juliet's affair with Romeo. She provides a contrast with Juliet, given that her view of love is earthy and sexual, whereas Juliet is idealistic and intense. The Nurse believes in love and wants Juliet to have a nice-looking husband, but the idea that Juliet would want to sacrifice herself for love is incomprehensible to her.

Tybalt A Capulet, Juliet's cousin on her mother's side. Vain, fashionable, supremely aware of courtesy and the lack of it, he becomes aggressive, violent, and quick to draw his sword when he feels his pride has been injured. Once drawn, his sword is something to be feared. He loathes Montagues.

Capulet The patriarch of the Capulet family, father of Juliet, husband of Lady Capulet, and enemy, for unexplained reasons, of Montague. He truly loves his daughter, though he is not well acquainted with Juliet's thoughts or feelings, and seems to think that what is best for her is a "good" match with Paris. Often prudent, he commands respect and propriety, but he is liable to fly into a rage when either is lacking.

Lady Capulet Juliet's mother, Capulet's wife. A woman who herself married young (by her own estimation she gave birth to Juliet at close to the age of fourteen), she is eager to see her daughter marry Paris. She is an ineffectual mother, relying on the Nurse for moral and pragmatic support.

Montague Romeo's father, the patriarch of the Montague clan and bitter enemy of Capulet. At the beginning of the play, he is chiefly concerned about Romeo's melancholy.

Lady Montague Romeo's mother, Montague's wife. She dies of grief after Romeo is exiled from Verona.

Paris A kinsman of the Prince, and the suitor of Juliet most preferred by Capulet. Once Capulet has promised him he can marry Juliet, he behaves very presumptuous toward her, acting as if they are already married.

Benvolio Montague's nephew, Romeo's cousin and thoughtful friend, he makes a genuine effort to defuse violent scenes in public places, though Mercutio accuses him of having a nasty temper in private. He spends most of the play trying to help Romeo get his mind off Rosaline, even after Romeo has fallen in love with Juliet.

Prince Escalus The Prince of Verona. A kinsman of Mercutio and Paris. As the seat of political power in Verona, he is concerned about maintaining the public peace at all costs.

Friar John A Franciscan friar charged by Friar Lawrence with taking the news of Juliet's false death to Romeo in Mantua. Friar John is held up in a quarantined house, and the message never reaches Romeo.

Balthasar Romeo's dedicated servant, who brings Romeo the news of Juliet's death, unaware that her death is a ruse.

Sampson & Gregory Two servants of the house of Capulet, who, like their master, hate the Montagues. At the outset of the play, they successfully provoke some Montague men into a fight.

Abram Montague's servant, who fights with Sampson and Gregory in the first scene of the play.

The Apothecary An apothecary in Mantua. Had he been wealthier, he might have been able to afford to value his morals more than money, and refused to sell poison to Romeo.

Peter A Capulet servant who invites guests to Capulet's feast and escorts the Nurse to meet with Romeo. He is illiterate, and a bad singer.

Rosaline The woman with whom Romeo is infatuated at the beginning of the play. Rosaline never appears onstage, but it is said by other characters that she is very beautiful and has sworn to live a life of chastity.

The Chorus The Chorus is a single character who, as developed in Greek drama, functions as a narrator offering commentary on the play's plot and themes.

Analysis of Major Characters

Romeo

The name Romeo, in popular culture, has become nearly synonymous with "lover." Romeo, in *Romeo and Juliet,* does indeed experience a love of such purity and passion that he kills himself when he believes that the object of his love, Juliet, has died. The power of Romeo's love, however, often obscures a clear vision of Romeo's character, which is far more complex.

Even Romeo's relation to love is not so simple. At the beginning of the play, Romeo pines for Rosaline, proclaiming her the paragon of women and despairing at her indifference toward him. Taken together, Romeo's Rosaline-induced histrionics seem rather juvenile. Romeo is a great reader of love poetry, and the portrayal of his love for Rosaline suggests he is trying to re-create the feelings that he has read about. After first kissing Juliet, she tells him "you kiss by th' book," meaning that he kisses according to the rules, and implying that while proficient, his kissing lacks originality (I.v.107). In reference to Rosaline, it seems, Romeo loves by the book. Rosaline, of course, slips from Romeo's mind at first sight of Juliet. But Juliet is no mere replacement. The love she shares with Romeo is far deeper, more authentic and unique than the clichéd puppy love Romeo felt for Rosaline. Romeo's love matures over the course of the play from the shallow desire to be in love to a profound and intense passion. One must ascribe Romeo's development at least in part to Juliet. Her level-headed observations, such as the one about Romeo's kissing, seem just the thing to snap Romeo from his superficial idea of love and to inspire him to begin to speak some of the most beautiful and intense love poetry ever written.

Yet Romeo's deep capacity for love is merely a part of his larger capacity for intense feeling of all kinds. Put another way, it is possible to describe Romeo as lacking the capacity for moderation. Love compels him to sneak into the garden of his enemy's daughter, risking death simply to catch a glimpse of her. Anger compels him to kill his wife's cousin in a reckless duel to avenge the death of his friend.

Despair compels him to suicide upon hearing of Juliet's death. Such extreme behavior dominates Romeo's character throughout the play and contributes to the ultimate tragedy that befalls the lovers. Had Romeo restrained himself from killing Tybalt, or waited even one day before killing himself after hearing the news of Juliet's death, matters might have ended happily. Of course, though, had Romeo not had such depths of feeling, the love he shared with Juliet would never have existed in the first place.

Among his friends, especially while bantering with Mercutio, Romeo shows glimpses of his social persona. He is intelligent, quick-witted, fond of verbal jousting (particularly about sex), loyal, and unafraid of danger.

Juliet

Having not quite reached her fourteenth birthday, Juliet is of an age that stands on the border between immaturity and maturity. At the play's beginning however she seems merely an obedient, sheltered, naïve child. Though many girls her age—including her mother—get married, Juliet has not given the subject any thought. When Lady Capulet mentions Paris's interest in marrying Juliet, Juliet dutifully responds that she will try to see if she can love him, a response that seems childish in its obedience and in its immature conception of love. Juliet seems to have no friends her own age, and she is not comfortable talking about sex (as seen in her discomfort when the Nurse goes on and on about a sexual joke at Juliet's expense in Act I, scene iii).

Juliet gives glimpses of her determination, strength, and sober-mindedness, in her earliest scenes, and offers a preview of the woman she will become during the four-day span of *Romeo and Juliet.* While Lady Capulet proves unable to quiet the Nurse, Juliet succeeds with one word (also in Act I, scene iii). In addition, even in Juliet's dutiful acquiescence to try to love Paris, there is some seed of steely determination. Juliet promises to consider Paris as a possible husband to the precise degree her mother desires. While an outward show of obedience, such a statement can also be read as a refusal through passivity. Juliet will accede to her mother's wishes, but she will not go out of her way to fall in love with Paris.

Juliet's first meeting with Romeo propels her full-force toward adulthood. Though profoundly in love with him, Juliet is able to see and criticize Romeo's rash decisions and his tendency to romanticize things. After Romeo kills Tybalt and is banished, Juliet does not follow him blindly. She makes a logical and heartfelt decision that her loyalty and love for Romeo must be her guiding priorities. Essentially, Juliet cuts herself loose from her prior social moorings—her nurse, her parents, and her social position in Verona—in order to try to reunite with Romeo. When she wakes in the tomb to find Romeo dead, she does not kill herself out of feminine weakness, but rather out of an intensity of love, just as Romeo did. Juliet's suicide actually requires more nerve than Romeo's: while he swallows poison, she stabs herself through the heart with a dagger.

Juliet's development from a wide-eyed girl into a self-assured, loyal, and capable woman is one of Shakespeare's early triumphs of characterization. It also marks one of his most confident and rounded treatments of a female character.

Friar Lawrence

Friar Lawrence occupies a strange position in *Romeo and Juliet*. He is a kindhearted cleric who helps Romeo and Juliet throughout the play. He performs their marriage and gives generally good advice, especially in regard to the need for moderation. He is the sole figure of religion in the play. But Friar Lawrence is also the most scheming and political of characters in the play: he marries Romeo and Juliet as part of a plan to end the civil strife in Verona; he spirits Romeo into Juliet's room and then out of Verona; he devises the plan to reunite Romeo and Juliet through the deceptive ruse of a sleeping potion that seems to arise from almost mystic knowledge. This mystical knowledge seems out of place for a Catholic friar; why does he have such knowledge, and what could such knowledge mean? The answers are not clear. In addition, though Friar Lawrence's plans all seem well conceived and well intentioned, they serve as the main mechanisms through which the fated tragedy of the play occurs. Readers should recognize that the Friar is not only subject to the fate that dominates the play—in many ways he brings that fate about.

Mercutio

With a lightning-quick wit and a clever mind, Mercutio is a scene stealer and one of the most memorable characters in all of Shakespeare's works. Though he constantly puns, jokes, and teases—

sometimes in fun, sometimes with bitterness—Mercutio is not a mere jester or prankster. With his wild words, Mercutio punctures the romantic sentiments and blind self-love that exist within the play. He mocks Romeos self-indulgence just as he ridicules Tybalt's hauteur and adherence to fashion. The critic Stephen Greenblatt describes Mercutio as a force within the play that functions to deflate the possibility of romantic love and the power of tragic fate. Unlike the other characters who blame their deaths on fate, Mercutio dies cursing all Montagues and Capulets. Mercutio believes that specific people are responsible for his death rather than some external impersonal force.

Themes, Motifs & Symbols

Themes

Themes are the fundamental and often universal ideas explored in a literary work.

The Forcefulness of Love

Romeo and Juliet is the most famous love story in the English literary tradition. Love is naturally the play's dominant and most important theme. The play focuses on romantic love, specifically the intense passion that springs up at first sight between Romeo and Juliet. In *Romeo and Juliet,* love is a violent, ecstatic, overpowering force that supersedes all other values, loyalties, and emotions. In the course of the play, the young lovers are driven to defy their entire social world: families ("Deny thy father and refuse thy name," Juliet asks, "Or if thou wilt not, be but sworn my love, / And I'll no longer be a Capulet"); friends (Romeo abandons Mercutio and Benvolio after the feast in order to go to Juliet's garden); and ruler (Romeo returns to Verona for Juliet's sake after being exiled by the Prince on pain of death in II.i.76–78). Love is the overriding theme of the play, but a reader should always remember that Shakespeare is uninterested in portraying a prettied-up, dainty version of the emotion, the kind that bad poets write about, and whose bad poetry Romeo reads while pining for Rosaline. Love in *Romeo and Juliet* is a brutal, powerful emotion that captures individuals and catapults them against their world, and, at times, against themselves.

The powerful nature of love can be seen in the way it is described, or, more accurately, the way descriptions of it so consistently fail to capture its entirety. At times love is described in the terms of religion, as in the fourteen lines when Romeo and Juliet first meet. At others it is described as a sort of magic: "Alike bewitchèd by the charm of looks" (II.Prologue.6). Juliet, perhaps, most perfectly describes her love for Romeo by refusing to describe it: "But my true love is grown to such excess / I cannot sum up some of half my wealth" (III.i.33–34). Love, in other

THEMES

words, resists any single metaphor because it is too powerful to be so easily contained or understood.

Romeo and Juliet does not make a specific moral statement about the relationships between love and society, religion, and family; rather, it portrays the chaos and passion of being in love, combining images of love, violence, death, religion, and family in an impressionistic rush leading to the play's tragic conclusion.

Love as a Cause of Violence

The themes of death and violence permeate *Romeo and Juliet,* and they are always connected to passion, whether that passion is love or hate. The connection between hate, violence, and death seems obvious. But the connection between love and violence requires further investigation.

Love, in *Romeo and Juliet,* is a grand passion, and as such it is blinding; it can overwhelm a person as powerfully and completely as hate can. The passionate love between Romeo and Juliet is linked from the moment of its inception with death: Tybalt notices that Romeo has crashed the feast and determines to kill him just as Romeo catches sight of Juliet and falls instantly in love with her. From that point on, love seems to push the lovers closer to love and violence, not farther from it. Romeo and Juliet are plagued with thoughts of suicide, and a willingness to experience it: in Act III, scene iii, Romeo brandishes a knife in Friar Lawrence's cell and threatens to kill himself after he has been banished from Verona and his love. Juliet also pulls a knife in order to take her own life in Friar Lawrence's presence just three scenes later. After Capulet decides that Juliet will marry Paris, Juliet says, "If all else fail, myself have power to die" (III.v.242). Finally, each imagines that the other looks dead the morning after their first, and only, sexual experience ("Methinks I see thee," Juliet says, ". . . as one dead in the bottom of a tomb" (III.v.55–56). This theme continues until its inevitable conclusion: double suicide. This tragic choice is the highest, most potent expression of love that Romeo and Juliet can make. It is only through death that they can preserve their love, and their love is so profound that they are willing to end their lives in its defense. In the play, love emerges as an amoral thing, leading as much to destruction as to happiness. But in its extreme passion, the love that Romeo and Juliet experience also appears so exquisitely beautiful that few would want, or be able, to resist its power.

The Individual Versus Society

Much of *Romeo and Juliet* involves the lovers' struggles against public and social institutions that either explicitly or implicitly oppose the existence of their love. Such structures range from the concrete to the abstract: families and the placement of familial power in the father; law and the desire for public order; religion; and the social importance placed on masculine honor. These institutions often come into conflict with each other. The importance of honor, for example, time and again results in brawls that disturb the public peace.

Though they do not always work in concert, each of these societal institutions in some way present obstacles for Romeo and Juliet. The enmity between their families, coupled with the emphasis placed on loyalty and honor to kin, combine to create a profound conflict for Romeo and Juliet, who must rebel against their heritages. Further, the patriarchal power structure inherent in Renaissance families, wherein the father controls the action of all other family members, particularly women, places Juliet in an extremely vulnerable position. Her heart, in her family's mind, is not hers to give. The law and the emphasis on social civility demands terms of conduct with which the blind passion of love cannot comply. Religion similarly demands priorities that Romeo and Juliet cannot abide by because of the intensity of their love. Though in most situations the lovers uphold the traditions of Christianity (they wait to marry before consummating their love), their love is so powerful that they begin to think of each other in blasphemous terms. For example, Juliet calls Romeo "the god of my idolatry," elevating Romeo to level of God (II.i.156). The couple's final act of suicide is likewise un-Christian. The maintenance of masculine honor forces Romeo to commit actions he would prefer to avoid. But the social emphasis placed on masculine honor is so profound that Romeo cannot simply ignore them.

It is possible to see *Romeo and Juliet* as a battle between the responsibilities and actions demanded by social institutions and those demanded by the private desires of the individual. Romeo and Juliet's appreciation of night, with its darkness and privacy, and their renunciation of their names, with its attendant loss of obligation, make sense in the context of individuals who wish to escape the public world. But the lovers cannot stop the night from becoming day. And Romeo cannot cease being a Montague simply because he wants to; the rest of the world will not let him. The lovers' suicides can be understood as the ultimate night, the ultimate privacy.

The Inevitability of Fate

In its first address to the audience, the Chorus states that Romeo and Juliet are "star-crossed"—that is to say that fate (a power often vested in the movements of the stars) controls them (Prologue.6). This sense of fate permeates the play, and not just for the audience. The characters also are quite aware of it: Romeo and Juliet constantly see omens. When Romeo believes that Juliet is dead, he cries out, "Then I defy you, stars," completing the idea that the love between Romeo and Juliet is in opposition to the decrees of destiny (V.i.24). Of course, Romeo's defiance itself plays into the hands of fate, and his determination to spend eternity with Juliet results in their deaths. The mechanism of fate works in all of the events surrounding the lovers: the feud between their families (it is worth noting that this hatred is never explained; rather, the reader must accept it as an undeniable aspect of the world of the play); the horrible series of accidents that ruin Friar Lawrence's seemingly well-intentioned plans at the end of the play; and the tragic timing of Romeo's suicide and Juliet's awakening. These events are not mere coincidences, but rather manifestations of fate that help bring about the unavoidable outcome of the young lovers' deaths.

The concept of fate described above is the most commonly accepted interpretation. There are other possible readings of fate in the play: as a force determined by the powerful social institutions that influence Romeo and Juliet's choices, as well as fate as a force that emerges from Romeo and Juliet's very personalities.

Motifs

Motifs are recurring structures, contrasts, and literary devices that can help to develop and inform the text's major themes.

Light/Dark Imagery

One of the play's most consistent visual motifs is the contrast between light and dark, often in terms of night/day imagery. This contrast is not given a particular metaphoric meaning—light is not always good, and dark is not always evil. On the contrary, light and dark are generally used to provide a sensory contrast and to hint at opposed alternatives. One of the more important instances of this motif is Romeo's lengthy meditation on the sun and the moon during the balcony scene, in which Juliet, metaphorically described as the sun, is seen as banishing the "envious moon" and transforming the night into day (II.i.46). A similar blurring of night and day occurs in the early morning hours after the lovers' only night together. Romeo, forced to leave for exile in the morning, and Juliet, not wanting him to leave her room, both try to pretend that it is still night, and that the light is actually darkness: "More light and light, more dark and dark our woes" (III.v.36).

Opposite Points of View

Shakespeare includes numerous speeches and scenes in Romeo and Juliet that hint at alternative ways to evaluate the play. Shakespeare uses two main devices in this regard: Mercutio and servants. Mercutio consistently skewers the viewpoints of all the other characters in play: he sees Romeo's devotion to love as a sort of blindness that robs Romeo from himself; similarly, he sees Tybalt's devotion to honor as blind and stupid. His punning and the Queen Mab speech can be interpreted as undercutting virtually every passion evident in the play. Mercutio serves as a critic of the delusions of righteousness and grandeur held by the characters around him.

Where Mercutio is a nobleman who openly criticizes other nobles, the views offered by servants in the play are less explicit. There is the Nurse who lost her baby and husband, the servant Peter who cannot read, the musicians who care about their lost wages and their lunches, and the Apothecary who cannot afford to make the moral choice, the lower classes present a second tragic world to counter that of the nobility. The nobles' world is full of grand tragic gestures. The servants' world, in contrast, is characterized by simple needs, and early deaths brought about by disease and poverty rather than dueling and grand passions. Where the nobility almost seem to revel in their capacity for drama, the servants' lives are such that they cannot afford tragedy of the epic kind.

Symbols

Symbols are objects, characters, figures, and colors used to represent abstract ideas or concepts.

Poison

In his first appearance, in Act II, scene ii, Friar Lawrence remarks that every plant, herb, and stone has its own special properties, and that nothing exists in nature that cannot be put to both good and bad uses. Thus, poison is not intrinsically evil, but is instead a natural substance made lethal by human hands. Friar Lawrence's words prove true over the course of the play. The sleeping potion he gives Juliet is concocted to cause the appearance of death, not death itself, but through circumstances beyond the Friar's control, the potion does bring about a fatal result: Romeo's suicide. As this example shows, human beings tend to cause death even without intending to. Similarly, Romeo suggests that society is to blame for the Apothecary's criminal selling of poison, because while there are laws prohibiting the apothecary from selling poison, there are no laws that would help the apothecary make money. Poison symbolizes human society's tendency to poison good things and make them fatal, just as the pointless Capulet-Montague feud turns Romeo and Juliet's love to poison. After all, unlike many of the other tragedies, this play does not have an evil villain, but rather people whose good qualities are turned to poison by the world in which they live.

Thumb-biting

In Act I, scene I, the buffoonish Samson begins a brawl between the Montagues and Capulets by flicking his thumbnail from behind his upper teeth, an insulting gesture known as biting the thumb. He engages in this juvenile and vulgar display because he wants to get into a fight with the Montagues but doesn't want to be accused of starting the fight by making an explicit insult. Because of his timidity, he settles for being annoying rather than challenging. The thumb-biting, as an essentially meaningless gesture, represents the foolishness of the entire Capulet/Montague feud and the stupidity of violence in general.

Queen Mab

In Act I, scene iv, Mercutio delivers a dazzling speech about the fairy Queen Mab, who rides through the night on her tiny wagon bringing dreams to sleepers. One of the most noteworthy aspects of Queen Mab's ride is that the dreams she brings generally do not bring out the best sides of the dreamers, but instead serve to confirm them in whatever vices they are addicted to—for example, greed, violence, or lust. Another important aspect of Mercutio's description of Queen Mab is that it is complete nonsense, albeit vivid and highly colorful. Nobody believes in a fairy pulled about by "a small grey-coated gnat" whipped with a cricket's bone (I.iv.65). Finally, it is worth noting that the description of Mab and her carriage goes to extravagant lengths to emphasize how tiny and insubstantial she and her accoutrements are. Queen Mab and her carriage do not merely symbolize the dreams of sleepers, they also symbolize the power of waking fantasies, daydreams, and desires. Through the Queen Mab imagery, Mercutio suggests that all desires and fantasies are as nonsensical and fragile as Mab, and that they are basically corrupting. This point of view contrasts starkly with that of Romeo and Juliet, who see their love as real and ennobling.

Summary & Analysis

Prologue

Summary

From forth the fatal loins of these two foes
A pair of star-crossed lovers take their life. . . .

As a prologue to the play, the Chorus enters. In a fourteen-line sonnet, the Chorus describes two noble households (called "houses") in the city of Verona. The houses hold an "ancient grudge" (Prologue.2) against each other that remains a source of violent and bloody conflict. The Chorus states that from these two houses, two "star-crossed" (Prologue.6) lovers will appear. These lovers will mend the quarrel between their families by dying. The story of these two lovers, and of the terrible strife between their families, will be the topic of this play.

Analysis

This opening speech by the Chorus serves as an introduction to *Romeo and Juliet*. We are provided with information about where the play takes place, and given some background information about its principal characters.

The obvious function of the Prologue as introduction to the Verona of *Romeo and Juliet* can obscure its deeper, more important function. The Prologue does not merely set the scene of *Romeo and Juliet*, it tells the audience exactly what is going to happen in the play. The Prologue refers to an ill-fated couple with its use of the word "star-crossed," which means, literally, against the stars. Stars were thought to control people's destinies. But the Prologue itself *creates* this sense of fate by providing the audience with the knowledge that Romeo and Juliet will die even before the play has begun. The audience therefore watches the play with the expectation that it must fulfill the terms set in the Prologue. The structure of the play itself is the fate from which Romeo and Juliet cannot escape.

Act I, scene 1

Summary

Sampson and Gregory, two servants of the house of Capulet, stroll through the streets of Verona. With bawdy banter, Sampson vents his hatred of the house of Montague. The two exchange punning remarks about physically conquering Montague men and sexually conquering Montague women. Gregory sees two Montague servants approaching, and discusses with Sampson the best way to provoke them into a fight without breaking the law. Sampson bites his thumb at the Montagues—a highly insulting gesture. A verbal confrontation quickly escalates into a fight. Benvolio, a kinsman to Montague, enters and draws his sword in an attempt to stop the confrontation. Tybalt, a kinsman to Capulet, sees Benvolio's drawn sword and draws his own. Benvolio explains that he is merely trying to keep the peace, but Tybalt professes a hatred for peace as strong as his hatred for Montagues, and attacks. The brawl spreads. A group of citizens bearing clubs attempts to restore the peace by beating down the combatants. Montague and Capulet enter, and only their wives prevent them from attacking one another. Prince Escalus arrives and commands the fighting stop on penalty of torture. The Capulets and Montagues throw down their weapons. The Prince declares the violence between the two families has gone on for too long, and proclaims a death sentence upon anyone who disturbs the civil peace again. He says that he will speak to Capulet and Montague more directly on this matter; Capulet exits with him, the brawlers disperse, and Benvolio is left alone with his uncle and aunt, Montague and Lady Montague.

Benvolio describes to Montague how the brawl started. Lady Montague asks whether Benvolio has seen her son, Romeo. Benvolio replies that he earlier saw Romeo pacing through a grove of sycamores outside the city; since Romeo seemed troubled, Benvolio did not speak to him. Concerned about their son, the Montagues tell Benvolio that Romeo has often been seen melancholy, walking alone among the sycamores. They add that they have tried to discover what troubles him, but have had no success. Benvolio sees Romeo approaching, and promises to find out the reason for his melancholy. The Montagues quickly depart.

Benvolio approaches his cousin. With a touch of sadness, Romeo tells Benvolio that he is in love with Rosaline, but that she does not return his feelings and has in fact sworn to live a life of chastity.

Benvolio counsels Romeo to forget her by gazing on other beauties, but Romeo contends that the woman he loves is the most beautiful of all. Romeo departs, assuring Benvolio that he cannot teach him to forget his love. Benvolio resolves to do just that.

Analysis

In an opening full of rousing action that is sure to capture the audience's attention (and designed partly for that purpose), Shakespeare provides all the background information needed to understand the world of the play. In the brawl, he portrays all of the layers of Veronese society, from those lowest in power, the servants, to the Prince who occupies the political and social pinnacle. He further provides excellent characterization of Benvolio as thoughtful and fearful of the law, Tybalt as a hothead, and Romeo as distracted and lovelorn, while showing the deep and long-standing hatred between the Montagues and Capulets. At the same time, Shakespeare establishes some of the major themes of the play. The opening of *Romeo and Juliet* is a marvel of economy, descriptive power, and excitement.

The origin of the brawl, rife as it is with sexual and physical bravado, introduces the important theme of masculine honor. Masculine honor does not function in the play as some sort of stoic indifference to pain or insult. In Verona, a man must defend his honor whenever it is transgressed against, whether verbally or physically. This concept of masculine honor exists through every layer of society in Verona, from the servants on up to the noblemen. It animates Samson and Gregory as much as it does Tybalt.

It is significant that the fight between the Montagues and Capulets erupts first among the servants. Readers of the play generally focus on the two great noble families, as they should. But do not overlook Shakespeare's inclusion of servants in the story: the perspectives of servants in *Romeo and Juliet* are often used to comment on the actions of their masters, and therefore, society. When servants appear in the play, don't just dismiss them as props meant to make the world of *Romeo and Juliet* look realistic. The things servants say often change the way we can look at the play, showing that while the Montagues and Capulets are gloriously tragic, they are also supremely privileged and stupid, since only the stupid would bring death upon themselves when there is no need for it. The prosaic cares of the lower classes display the difficulty of their lives; a difficulty that the Capulets and Montagues would not have to face were they not so blinded by honor and hatred.

In the figures of the civil watch and the Prince, the brawl introduces the audience to a different aspect of the social world of Verona that exists beyond the Montagues and Capulets. This social world stands in constant contrast to the passions inherent in the Capulets and Montagues. The give-and-take between the demands of the social world and individuals' private passions is another powerful theme in the play. For example, look at how the servants try to attain their desire while remaining on the right side of the law. Note how careful Samson is to ask, "Is the law on our side, if I say 'Ay,'" before insulting the Montagues (I.i.42). After the prince institutes the death penalty for any who disturb the peace again, the stakes for letting private passions overwhelm public sobriety are raised to a new level.

Finally, this first scene also introduces us to Romeo the lover. But that introduction comes with a bit of a shock. In a play called *Romeo and Juliet* we would expect the forlorn Romeo to be lovesick over Juliet. But instead he is in love with Rosaline. Who is Rosaline? The question lingers through the play. She never appears onstage, but many of Romeo's friends, unaware that he has fallen in love with and married Juliet, believe he is in love with Rosaline for the entirety of the play. And Friar Lawrence, for one, expresses shock that Romeo's affections could shift so quickly from Rosaline to Juliet. In this way, Rosaline haunts *Romeo and Juliet*. One can argue that Rosaline exists in the play only to demonstrate Romeo's passionate nature, his love of love. For example, in the clichés he spouts about his love for Rosaline: "Feather of lead, bright smoke, cold fire, sick health" (I.i.173). It seems that Romeo's love for chaste Rosaline stems almost entirely from the reading of bad love poetry. Romeo's love for Rosaline, then, seems an immature love, more a statement that he is ready to be in love than actual love. An alternative argument holds that Romeo's love for Rosaline shows him to be desirous of love with anyone who is beautiful and willing to share his feelings, thereby sullying our understanding of Romeo's love with Juliet. Over the course of the play, the purity and power of Romeo's love for Juliet seems to outweigh any concerns about the origin of that love, and therefore any concerns about Rosaline, but the question of Rosaline's role in the play does offer an important point for consideration.

Act I, scene ii

Summary

On another street of Verona, Capulet walks with Paris, a noble kinsman of the Prince. The two discuss Paris's desire to marry Capulet's daughter, Juliet. Capulet is overjoyed, but also states that Juliet—not yet fourteen—is too young to get married. He asks Paris to wait two years. He assures Paris that he favors him as a suitor, and invites Paris to the traditional masquerade feast he is holding that very night so that Paris might begin to woo Juliet and win her heart. Capulet dispatches a servant, Peter, to invite a list of people to the feast. As Capulet and Paris walk away, Peter laments that he cannot read and will therefore have difficulty accomplishing his task.

Romeo and Benvolio happen by, still arguing about whether Romeo will be able to forget his love. Peter asks Romeo to read the list to him; Rosaline's name is one of those on the list. Before departing, Peter invites Romeo and Benvolio to the party—assuming, he says, that they are not Montagues. Benvolio tells Romeo that the feast will be the perfect opportunity to compare Rosaline with the other beautiful women of Verona. Romeo agrees to go with him, but only because Rosaline herself will be there.

Analysis

This scene introduces Paris as Capulet's pick for Juliet's husband and also sets into motion Romeo and Juliet's eventual meeting at the feast. In the process, the scene establishes how Juliet is subject to parental influence. Romeo might be forced into fights because of his father's enmity with the Capulets, but Juliet is far more constrained. Regardless of any inter-family strife, Juliet's father can force her to marry whomever he wants. Such is the difference between being a man and woman in Verona. It might seem a worse thing to be caught up in the violence of a brawl, but Juliet's status as a young woman leaves her with no power or choice in any social situation. Like any other female in this culture, she will be passed from the control of one man to another. In this scene, Capulet appears to be a kind-hearted man. He defers to Juliet's ability to choose for herself ("My will to her consent is but a part" [I.ii.15]). But his power to force her into a marriage if he feels it necessary is implicitly present. Thus parental influence in this tragedy becomes a tool of fate: Juliet's arranged marriage with Paris, and the traditional feud between Capulets and Montagues, will eventually contribute to the deaths of Romeo and Juliet. The forces that determine their fate are laid in place well before Romeo and Juliet even meet.

The specter of parental influence evident in this scene should itself be understood as an aspect of the force wielded over individuals by social structures such as family, religion, and politics. All of these massive social structures will, in time, throw obstacles in the path of Romeo and Juliet's love.

Peter, who cannot read, offers a touch of humor to this scene, especially in the way his illiteracy leads him to invite two Montagues to the party while expressly stating that no Montagues are invited. But Peter's poor education is also part of the entrenched social structures. Juliet has no power because she is a woman. Peter has no power because he is a lowly servant and therefore cannot read.

Romeo, of course, is still lovelorn for Rosaline; but the audience can tell at this point that Romeo will meet Juliet at the feast, and expectations begin to rise. Through Shakespeare's ingenious manipulation of the plot, the audience starts to feel the rustlings of approaching fate.

Act I, scene iii

Summary

In Capulet's house, just before the feast is to begin, Lady Capulet calls to the Nurse, needing help to find her daughter. Juliet enters, and Lady Capulet dismisses the Nurse so that she might speak with her daughter alone. She immediately changes her mind, however, and asks the Nurse to remain and add her counsel. Before Lady Capulet can begin to speak, the Nurse launches into a long story about how, as a child, an uncomprehending Juliet became an innocent accomplice to a sexual joke. Lady Capulet tries unsuccessfully to stop the wildly amused Nurse. An embarrassed Juliet forcefully commands that the Nurse stop.

Lady Capulet asks Juliet what she thinks about getting married. Juliet replies that she has not given it any thought. Lady Capulet observes that she gave birth to Juliet when she was almost Juliet's current age. She excitedly continues that Juliet must begin to think about marriage because the "valiant Paris" has expressed an interest in her (I.iii.76). Juliet dutifully replies that she will look upon Paris at the feast to see if she might love him. A servingman enters to announce the beginning of the feast.

ANALYSIS

Three scenes into the play, the audience finally meets the second title character. Thematically, this scene continues to develop the issue of parental influence, particularly the strength of that influence over girls. Lady Capulet, herself a woman who married at a young age, offers complete support for her husband's plan for their daughter, and puts pressure on Juliet to think about Paris as a husband before Juliet has begun to think about marriage at all. Juliet admits just how powerful the influence of her parents is when she says of Paris: "I'll look to like, looking liking move; / But no more deep will I endart mine eye / Than your consent gives strength to make it fly" (I.iii.100–101). In effect, Juliet is saying that she will follow her mother's advice exactly in thinking about Paris.

While providing a humorous moment, the Nurse's silly anecdote about Juliet as a baby also helps to portray the inevitability of Juliet's situation. The Nurse's husband's comment about Juliet falling on her back when she comes of age is a reference to Juliet one day engaging in the act of sex. His comment, therefore, shows that Juliet has been viewed as a potential object of sexuality and marriage since she was a toddler. In broad terms, Juliet's fate to someday be given away in marriage has been set since birth.

Beyond thematic development, this scene provides magnificent insight into the three main female characters. Lady Capulet is a flighty, ineffectual mother: she dismisses the Nurse, seeking to speak alone with her daughter, but as soon as the Nurse begins to depart, Lady Capulet becomes nervous and calls the Nurse back. The Nurse, in her hilarious inability to stop telling the story about her husband's innuendo about Juliet's sexual development, shows a vulgar streak, but also a familiarity with Juliet that implies that it was she, and not Lady Capulet, who raised the girl. Indeed, it was the Nurse, and not Lady Capulet, who suckled Juliet as a baby (I.iii.70).

Juliet herself is revealed in this scene as a rather naïve young girl who is obedient to her mother and the Nurse. But there are glimpses of a strength and intelligence in Juliet that are wholly absent in her mother. Where Lady Capulet cannot get the Nurse to cease with her story, Juliet stops it with a word. We noted already that Juliet's phrase "But no more deep will I endart mine eye / Than your consent gives strength to make it fly" seems to imply a complete acquiescence to her mother's control. But the phrase can also be interpreted as illustrating an effort on Juliet's part to use vague language as a means of asserting some control over her situation. In this phrase, while agreeing to see if she might be able to love Paris, she is at the same time saying that she will put no more enthusiasm into this effort than her mother demands. The phrase can therefore be interpreted as a sort of passive resistance.

In this scene once again a direct comparison is drawn between servants and masters. In the course of the Nurse's story it becomes clear that her own daughter, who would be Juliet's age, died long ago. The Nurse's husband also has died. These deaths might simply be coincidental, but it seems just as likely that they correspond to the Nurse's lower station in life.

Act I, scene iv

Summary

O, then I see Queen Mab has been with you. . . .
She is the fairies' midwife. . . .

(*See* QUOTATIONS, *p. 61*)

Romeo, Benvolio, and their friend Mercutio, all wearing masks, have gathered with a group of mask-wearing guests on their way to the Capulets' feast. Still melancholy, Romeo wonders how they will get into the Capulets' feast, since they are Montagues. When that concern is brushed aside, he states that he will not dance at the feast. Mercutio begins to gently mock Romeo, transforming all of Romeo's statements about love into blatantly sexual metaphors. Romeo refuses to engage in this banter, explaining that in a dream he learned that going to the feast was a bad idea. Mercutio responds with a long speech about Queen Mab of the fairies, who visits people's dreams. The speech begins as a flight of fancy, but Mercutio becomes almost entranced by it, and a bitter, fervent strain creeps in. Romeo steps in to stop the speech and calm Mercutio down. Mercutio admits that he has been talking of nothing, noting that dreams are but "the children of an idle brain" (I.iv.97).

Benvolio refocuses their attention on actually getting to the feast. Romeo voices one last concern: he has a feeling that the night's activities will set in motion the action of fate, resulting in untimely death. But, putting himself in the hands of "he who hath the steerage of my course," Romeo's spirits rise, and he continues with his friends toward the feast (I.iv.112).

ANALYSIS

This scene might seem unnecessary. As an audience, we already know that Romeo and his friends are headed to the feast. We already know that Romeo is melancholy and Benvolio more pragmatic. The inclusion of this scene does not directly offer plot exposition or plot progression.

However, the scene does augment the general sense of fate through Romeo's statement of belief that the night's events will lead to untimely death. The audience, of course, knows that he will suffer an untimely death. When Romeo gives himself up to "he that hath the steerage of my course," the audience feels fate take a tighter grasp on him (I.iv.112).

This scene also serves as introduction to the clever, whirling, entrancing Mercutio. Spinning wild puns left and right, seeming to speak them as freely as others breathe, Mercutio is established as a friend who can, gently or not, mock Romeo as no one else can. Though thoughtful, Benvolio does not have the quick wit for such behavior. With his wild speech and laughter, Mercutio is a man of excess. But his passions are of another sort than those that move Romeo to love and Tybalt to hate. Romeo's and Tybalt's passions are founded upon the acceptance of two different ideals trumpeted by society: the poetic tradition of love and the importance of honor. Mercutio believes in neither. In fact, Mercutio stands in contrast to all of the other characters in *Romeo and Juliet* because he is able to see through the blindness caused by wholehearted acceptance of the ideals sanctioned by society: he pokes holes in Romeo's rapturous adoption of the rhetoric of love just as he mocks Tybalt's fastidious adherence to the fashions of the day. It is no accident that Mercutio is the master punner in this play. A pun represents slippage, or twist, in the meaning of a word. That word, which previously meant one thing, now suddenly is revealed to have additional interpretations, and therefore becomes ambiguous. Just as Mercutio can see through words to other, usually debased meanings, he can also understand that the ideals held by those around him originate from less high-minded desires than anyone would care to admit.

Mercutio's Queen Mab speech is one of the most famous in the play. Queen Mab, who brings dreams to sleeping people, seems to be loosely based on figures in the pagan Celtic mythology that predated Christianity's arrival in England. Yet the name holds a deeper meaning. The words "quean" and "mab" were references to whores in Elizabethan England. In Queen Mab, then, Mercutio creates a sort of conceptual pun: he alludes to a mythological tradition peopled with fairies and attaches it to a reference to prostitutes. He yokes the childish fun of fairies to a much darker vision of humanity. The speech itself reveals this dichotomy. A child would love Mercutio's description of a world of fairies replete with walnut carriages and insect steeds, its stories of a fairy bringing dreams to sleeping people. But take a closer look at those dreams. Queen Mab brings dreams suited to each individual, and each dream she brings seems to descend into deeper depravity and brutality: lovers dream of love; lawyers dream of law cases and making money; soldiers dream of "cutting foreign throats" (I.iv.83). By the end of the speech, Queen Mab is the "hag" who teaches maidens to have sex. The child's fairy tale has spun into something much, much darker, though this dark vision is an accurate portrayal of society.

Mercutio, as entertaining as he is, can be seen as offering an alternative vision of the grand tragedy that is *Romeo and Juliet*. "Thou talk'st of nothing," Romeo says to Mercutio in order to force Mercutio to end the Queen Mab speech (I.iv.96). Mercutio agrees, saying that dreams "are the children of an idle brain" (I.iv.98). But don't Romeo's visions of love qualify as dreams? Don't Tybalt's fantasies of perfect proprietary and social standing count as dreams? And what about Friar Lawrence's dreams of bringing peace to Verona? In Mercutio's assessment, all of these desires "are the children of an idle brain." All are delusions. Mercutio's comment can be seen as a single pinprick in the grand idealistic passions of love and family loyalty that animate the play. The Queen Mab speech by no means deflates the great tragedy and romantic ideals of *Romeo and Juliet*, but it adds to them the subtext of a pun, that dark flipside which offers an alternative view of reality.

Act I, scene v

Summary

In the great hall of the Capulets, all is a-bustle. The servants work feverishly to make sure all runs smoothly, and set aside some food to make sure they have some enjoyment of the feast as well. Capulet makes his rounds through groups of guests, joking with them and encouraging all to dance.

From across the room, Romeo sees Juliet, and asks a servingman who she is. The servingman does not know. Romeo is transfixed;

Rosaline vanishes from his mind and he declares that he has never been in love until this moment. Moving through the crowd, Tybalt hears and recognizes Romeo's voice. Realizing that there is a Montague present, Tybalt sends a servant to fetch his rapier. Capulet overhears Tybalt and reprimands him, telling him that Romeo is well regarded in Verona, and that he will not have the youth harmed at his feast. Tybalt protests, but Capulet scolds him until he agrees to keep the peace. As Capulet moves on, Tybalt vows that he will not let this indignity pass.

Meanwhile, Romeo has approached Juliet and touched her hand. In a dialogue laced with religious metaphors that figure Juliet as a saint and Romeo as a pilgrim who wishes to erase his sin, he tries to convince her to kiss him, since it is only through her kiss that he might be absolved. Juliet agrees to remain still as Romeo kisses her. Thus, in the terms of their conversation, she takes his sin from him. Juliet then makes the logical leap that if she has taken Romeo's sin from him, his sin must now reside in her lips, and so they must kiss again.

Just as their second kiss ends, the Nurse arrives and tells Juliet that her mother wants to speak with her. Romeo asks the Nurse who Juliet's mother is. The Nurse replies that Lady Capulet is her mother. Romeo is devastated. As the crowd begins to disperse, Benvolio shows up and leads Romeo from the feast. Juliet is just as struck with the mysterious man she has kissed as Romeo is with her. She comments to herself that if he is already married, she feels she will die (I.v.131). In order to find out Romeo's identity without raising any suspicions, she asks the Nurse to identify a series of young men. The Nurse goes off and returns with the news that the man's name is Romeo, and that he is a Montague. Overcome with anguish that she loves a Montague, Juliet follows her nurse from the hall.

Analysis

This is the moment we've all been waiting for. Romeo sees Juliet and forgets Rosaline entirely; Juliet meets Romeo and falls just as deeply in love. The meeting of Romeo and Juliet dominates the scene, and, with extraordinary language that captures both the excitement and wonder that the two protagonists feel, Shakespeare proves equal to the expectations he has set up by delaying the meeting for an entire act.

The first conversation between Romeo and Juliet is an extended Christian metaphor. Using this metaphor, Romeo ingeniously manages to convince Juliet to let him kiss her. But the metaphor holds many further functions. The religious overtones of the conversation clearly imply that their love can be described only through the vocabulary of religion, that pure association with God. In this way, their love becomes associated with the purity and passion of the divine. But there is another side to this association of personal love and religion. In using religious language to describe their burgeoning feelings for each other, Romeo and Juliet tiptoe on the edge of blasphemy. Romeo compares Juliet to an image of a saint that should be worshiped, a role that Juliet is willing to play. Whereas the Catholic church held that the worship of saint's images was acceptable, the Anglican church of Elizabethan times saw it as blasphemy, a kind of idol worship. Romeo's statements about Juliet border on the heretical. Juliet commits an even more profound blasphemy in the next scene when she calls Romeo the "god of her idolatry," effectively installing Romeo in God's place in her personal religion (II.i.156). We have discussed already how Romeo and Juliet's love seems always to be opposed by the social structures of family, honor, and the civil desire for order. Here it is also shown to have some conflict, at least theologically, with religion.

When Romeo and Juliet meet they speak just fourteen lines before their first kiss. These fourteen lines make up a shared sonnet, with a rhyme scheme of ababcdcdefefgg. A sonnet is a perfect, idealized poetic form often used to write about love. Encapsulating the moment of origin of Romeo and Juliet's love within a sonnet therefore creates a perfect match between literary content and formal style. The use of the sonnet, however, also serves a second, darker purpose. The play's Prologue also is a single sonnet of the same rhyme scheme as Romeo and Juliet's shared sonnet. If you remember, the Prologue sonnet introduces the play, and, through its description of Romeo and Juliet's eventual death, also helps to create the sense of fate that permeates *Romeo and Juliet*. The shared sonnet between Romeo and Juliet therefore creates a formal link between their love and their destiny. With a single sonnet, Shakespeare finds a means of expressing perfect love and linking it to a tragic fate.

That fate begins to assert itself in the instant when Romeo and Juliet first meet: Tybalt recognizes Romeo's voice when Romeo first exclaims at Juliet's beauty. Capulet, acting cautiously, stops Tybalt from taking immediate action, but Tybalt's rage is set, creating the circumstances that will eventually banish Romeo from Verona. In the meeting between Romeo and Juliet lie the seeds of their shared tragedy.

The first conversation between Romeo and Juliet also provides a glimpse of the roles that each will play in their relationship. In this scene, Romeo is clearly the aggressor. He uses all the skill at his disposal to win over a struck, but timid, Juliet. Note that Juliet does not move during their first kiss; she simply lets Romeo kiss her. She is still a young girl, and though already in her dialogue with Romeo has proved herself intelligent, she is not ready to throw herself into action. But Juliet is the aggressor in the second kiss. It is *her* logic that forces Romeo to kiss her again and take back the sin he has placed upon her lips. In a single conversation, Juliet transforms from a proper, timid young girl to one more mature, who understands what she desires and is quick-witted enough to procure it. Juliet's subsequent comment to Romeo, "You kiss by th' book," can be taken in two ways (I.v.107). First, it can be seen as emphasizing Juliet's lack of experience. Many productions of *Romeo and Juliet* have Juliet say this line with a degree of wonder, so that the words mean "you are an *incredible* kisser, Romeo." But it is possible to see a bit of wry observation in this line. Juliet's comment that Romeo kisses by the book is akin to noting that he kisses as if he has learned how to kiss from a manual and followed those instructions exactly. In other words, he is proficient, but unoriginal (note that Romeo's love for Rosaline is described in exactly these terms, as learned from reading books of romantic poetry). Juliet is clearly smitten with Romeo, but it is possible to see her as the more incisive of the two, and as nudging Romeo to a more genuine level of love through her observation of his tendency to get caught up in the forms of love rather than love itself.

Act II, prologue–scene i

Summary: Act II, prologue

The Chorus delivers another short sonnet describing the new love between Romeo and Juliet: the hatred between the lovers' families makes it difficult for them to find the time or place to meet and let their passion grow; but the prospect of their love gives each of them the power and determination to elude the obstacles placed in their path.

Summary: Act II, scene i

But soft, what light through yonder window breaks?
It is the east, and Juliet is the sun.

(See QUOTATIONS, *p. 59)*

Having left the feast, Romeo decides that he cannot go home. He must instead try to find Juliet. He climbs a wall bordering the Capulet property and leaps down into the Capulet orchard. Benvolio and Mercutio enter, calling out for Romeo. They are sure he is nearby, but Romeo does not answer. Exasperated and amused, Mercutio mocks Romeo's feelings for Rosaline in an obscene speech. Mercutio and Benvolio exit under the assumption that Romeo does not want to be found. In the orchard, Romeo hears Mercutio's teasing. He says to himself, "He jests at scars that never felt a wound" (II.i.43).

Juliet suddenly appears at a window above the spot where Romeo is standing. Romeo compares her to the morning sun, far more beautiful than the moon it banishes. He nearly speaks to her, but thinks better of it. Juliet, musing to herself and unaware that Romeo is in her garden, asks why Romeo must be Romeo—a Montague, and therefore an enemy to her family. She says that if he would refuse his Montague name, she would give herself to him; or if he would simply swear that he loved her, she would refuse her Capulet name. Romeo responds to her plea, surprising Juliet, since she thought she was alone. She wonders how he found her and he tells her that love led him to her. Juliet worries that Romeo will be murdered if he is found in the garden, but Romeo refuses to budge, claiming that Juliet's love would make him immune to his enemies. Juliet admits she feels as strongly about Romeo as he professes he loves her, but she worries that perhaps Romeo will prove inconstant or false, or will think Juliet too easily won. Romeo begins to swear to her, but she stops him, concerned that everything is happening too quickly. He reassures her, and the two confess their love again. The Nurse calls for Juliet, and Juliet goes inside for a moment. When she reappears, she tells Romeo that she will send someone to him the next day to see if his love is honorable and if he intends to wed her. The Nurse calls again, and again Juliet withdraws. She appears at the window once more to set a time when her emissary should call on him: they settle on nine in the morning. They exult in their love for another moment before saying good night. Juliet goes back inside her chamber, and Romeo departs in search of a monk to aid him in his cause.

> *O Romeo, Romeo,*
> *wherefore art thou Romeo?*

(See QUOTATIONS, *p. 60)*

ANALYSIS: ACT II, PROLOGUE–SCENE I

The prologue to the second act reinforces themes that have already appeared. One love has been replaced by another through the enchanting power of the "charm of looks," and the force of parental influence stands in the way of the lovers' happiness. This prologue functions less as the voice of fate than the first one does. Instead it builds suspense by laying out the problem of the two lovers and hinting that there may be some way to overcome it: "But passion lends them power, time means, to meet, / Temp'ring extremities with extreme sweet" (II.Prologue.13–14).

Act II is the happiest and least tragic act in the play. In it, Shakespeare devotes himself to exploring the positive, joyful, and romantic aspects of young love. Scene i, the balcony scene (so called because it is often staged with Juliet on a balcony, though the stage directions suggest only that she is at a window above Romeo), is one of the most famous scenes in all of theater, owing to its beautiful and evocative poetry. Shakespeare plumbs the depths of the young lovers' characters, and captures the subtleties of their interaction, as in Juliet's struggle between the need for caution and an overpowering desire to be with Romeo.

Many of the most important scenes in *Romeo and Juliet,* such as the balcony scene, take place either very late at night or very early in the morning, since Shakespeare must use the full length of each day in order to compress the action of the play into just four days. Shakespeare exploits the transition between day and night with a recurring light/dark motif, sometimes drawing a sharp distinction between night and day, at other times blurring the boundaries between them. Romeo's long, impassioned description of Juliet in the balcony scene is an example of this theme. Romeo imagines that Juliet is the sun, rising from the east to banish the night; in effect, he says that she is transforming night into day.

Romeo is of course speaking metaphorically here; Juliet is not the sun, and it is still night in the orchard. But Romeo states the comparison with such devotion that it should be clear to the audience that, for him, it is no simple metaphor. For Romeo, Juliet is the sun, and it is no longer night. Here is an example of the power of language to briefly transform the world, in the service of love.

And yet, in the same speech, Romeo and Juliet also question the power of language. Wishing that Romeo were not the son of her father's enemy, Juliet says:

'Tis but thy name that is my enemy.
Thou art thyself, though not a Montague.
What's Montague? It is nor hand, nor foot,

Nor arm, nor face, nor any other part
Belonging to a man. O, be some other name!
What's in a name? That which we call a rose
By any other word would smell as sweet.
(II.i.80–86)

Here Juliet questions why Romeo must be her enemy. She refuses to believe that Romeo is defined by being a Montague, and therefore implies that the two of them can love each other without fear of the social repercussions. But language as an expression of social institutions such as family, politics, or religion cannot be dismissed so easily because no other character in the play is willing to dismiss them. Juliet loves Romeo because he is Romeo, but the power of her love cannot remove from him his last name of Montague or all that it stands for. In the privacy of the garden the language of love is triumphant. But in the social world, the language of society holds sway. This battle of language, in which Romeo and Juliet try to remake the world so that it would allow for their love, is one to keep an eye on.

Act II, scenes ii–iii

Summary: Act II, scene ii

In the early morning, Friar Lawrence enters, holding a basket. He fills the basket with various weeds, herbs, and flowers. While musing on the beneficence of the Earth, he demonstrates a deep knowledge of the properties of the plants he collects. Romeo enters and Friar Lawrence intuits that Romeo has not slept the night before. The friar fears that Romeo may have slept in sin with Rosaline. Romeo assures him that did not happen, and describes his new love for Juliet, his intent to marry her, and his desire that the friar consent to marry them that very day. Friar Lawrence is shocked at this sudden shift from Rosaline to Juliet. He comments on the fickleness of young love, Romeo's in particular. Romeo defends himself, noting that Juliet returns his love while Rosaline did not. In response, the friar comments that Rosaline could see that Romeo's love for her "did read by rote, that could not spell." Remaining skeptical at Romeo's sudden change of heart, Friar Lawrence nonetheless agrees to marry the couple. He expresses the hope that the marriage of Romeo and Juliet might end the feud ravaging the Montagues and Capulets.

Summary: Act II, scene iii

Later that morning, just before nine, Mercutio and Benvolio wonder what happened to Romeo the previous night. Benvolio has learned from a Montague servant that Romeo did not return home; Mercutio spouts some unkind words about Rosaline. Benvolio also relates that Tybalt has sent a letter to Romeo challenging him to a duel. Mercutio responds that Romeo is already dead, struck by Cupid's arrow; he wonders aloud whether Romeo is man enough to defeat Tybalt. When Benvolio comes to Romeo's defense, Mercutio launches into an extended description of Tybalt. He describes Tybalt as a master swordsman, perfectly proper and composed in style. According to Mercutio, however, Tybalt is also a vain, affected "fashionmonger" (II.iii.29). Mercutio disdains all that Tybalt stands for.

Romeo arrives. Mercutio immediately begins to ridicule him, claiming that Romeo has been made weak by love. As a way of mocking what he believes is Romeo's overwrought love for Rosaline, Mercutio takes the part of Romeo and compares Rosaline to all the most famous beauties of antiquity, finding Rosaline far superior. Then Mercutio accuses Romeo of abandoning his friends the previous night. Romeo does not deny the charge, but claims his need was great, and so the offense is forgivable. From this proceeds intricate, witty, and wildly sexual verbal jousting.

The Nurse enters, trailed by the servant, Peter. The Nurse asks if any of the three young men know Romeo, and Romeo identifies himself. Mercutio teases the Nurse, insinuating that she is a harlot, thus infuriating her. Benvolio and Mercutio take their leave to have dinner at Montague's house, and Romeo says he will follow shortly. The Nurse warns Romeo that he had better not attempt to "deal double" with Juliet, and Romeo assures her he is not. He asks the Nurse to tell Juliet to find some way to attend confession at Friar Lawrence's cell that afternoon; there they will be married. The Nurse agrees to deliver the message. The Nurse also agrees to set up a cloth ladder so that Romeo might ascend to Juliet's room on their wedding night.

Analysis: Act II, scenes ii–iii

In this scene we are introduced to Friar Lawrence as he meditates on the duality of good and evil that exists in all things. Speaking of medicinal plants, the friar claims that, though everything in nature has a useful purpose, it can also lead to misfortune if used improperly:

"For naught so vile that on the earth doth live / But to the earth some special good doth give, / Nor aught so good but strain'd from that fair use / Revolts from true birth, stumbling on abuse: / Virtue itself turns vice, being misapplied; / And vice sometime's by action dignified" (II.ii.17–22). At the end of this passage, the friar's rumination turns toward a broader application; he speaks of how good may be perverted to evil and evil may be purified by good. The friar tries to put his theories to use when he agrees to marry Romeo and Juliet; he hopes that the good of their love will reverse the evil of the hatred between the feuding families. Unfortunately, he later causes the flipside of his theory to come into play: the plan involving a sleep-inducing potion, which he intends to preserve Romeo and Juliet's marriage and love, results in both of their deaths.

The thematic role of the friar in *Romeo and Juliet* is hard to pin down. Clearly, Friar Lawrence is a kindhearted friend to both Romeo and Juliet. He also seems wise and selfless. But while the friar appears to embody all these good qualities that are often associated with religion, he is also an unknowing servant of fate: all of his plans go awry and create the misunderstandings that lead to the final tragedy.

Friar Lawrence also returns the specter of Rosaline to the play. The friar cannot believe that Romeo's love could turn so quickly from one person to another. Romeo's response, that Juliet returns his love while Rosaline did not, hardly provides evidence that Romeo has matured. The question of Rosaline continues on into the next scene when Mercutio begins to ridicule Romeo's lovelorn ways by mockingly comparing Rosaline to all the beauties of antiquity (it is interesting to note that one of these beauties, Thisbe, is found in a myth that very closely resembles the plot of *Romeo and Juliet*). The events of the play prove Romeo's steadfast love for Juliet, but Romeo's immature love for Rosaline, his love of love, is never quite erased. He remains too quick to follow the classic examples of love, up to and including his suicide.

In addition to developing the plot by which Romeo and Juliet will wed, Act II, scene iii offers a glimpse of Romeo among his friends. Romeo shows himself to be as proficient and bawdy a punner as Mercutio. This punning Romeo is what Mercutio believes to be the "true" Romeo, suddenly freed from the ludicrous melancholy of love: "Why, is not this better than groaning for love? / Now art thou sociable, now art thou Romeo" (II.iii.76-77). In the last scene, Juliet tried to battle the social world through the power of her private love; here Mercutio tries to assert the social language of male bravado and banter over the private introspection of love. Interestingly, both Juliet and Mercutio think they know the "real" Romeo. A conflict emerges; even friendship stands in opposition to Romeo's love. Romeo must remain both the private lover and the public Montague and friend, and he must somehow find a way to navigate between the different claims that his two roles demand of him.

Act II, scenes iv–v

Summary: Act II, scene iv

In the Capulet orchard, Juliet impatiently waits for her nurse, whom she sent to meet Romeo three hours earlier. At last the Nurse returns, and Juliet anxiously presses her for news. The Nurse claims to be too tired, sore, and out of breath to tell Juliet what has happened. Juliet grows frantic, and eventually the Nurse gives in and tells her that Romeo is waiting at Friar Lawrence's cell to marry her. The Nurse departs to wait in the ally for Romeo's servant, who is to bring a ladder for Romeo to use to climb up to Juliet's chamber that night to consummate their marriage.

Summary: Act II, scene v

Romeo and Friar Lawrence wait for Juliet to arrive at the cell. An ecstatic Romeo brashly states that he does not care what misfortune might come, as it will pale in comparison to the joy he feels right now. Friar Lawrence counsels Romeo to love moderately and not with too much intensity, saying, "these violent delights have violent ends" (II.v.9). Juliet enters and Romeo asks her to speak poetically of her love. Juliet responds that those who can so easily describe their "worth" are beggars, her love is far too great to be so easily described. The lovers exit with Friar Lawrence and are wed.

Analysis: Act II, scenes iv–v

Throughout these scenes, Shakespeare emphasizes the thrilling joy of young, romantic love. Romeo and Juliet are electric with anticipation. In a wonderfully comic scene, Juliet can barely contain herself when the Nurse pretends to be too tired to give her the news. Romeo is equally excited, brashly and blasphemously proclaiming his love is the most powerful force in the world.

Though the euphoria of love clearly dominates these scenes, some ominous foreshadowing is revealed. The Nurse's joking game in which she delays telling Juliet the news will find its sad mirror in a future scene, when the Nurse's anguish prevents her from relating news to Juliet and thereby causing terrible confusion. A more profound foreshadowing exists in the friar's observation, in reference to Romeo's powerful love, that "these violent delights have violent ends" (II.v.9). Every audience member knows that the play is a tragedy, and that Romeo and Juliet will die. The friar's words therefore are more than just a difference of opinion with Romeo; they reinforce the presence and power of fate.

Friar Lawrence's devotion to moderation is interesting in that it offers an alternative to the way in which all the other characters in *Romeo and Juliet* live their lives. From Romeo to Tybalt, and Montague to Capulet, every character follows passion, forsakes moderation. The friar criticizes this way of acting and feeling, noting its destructiveness. Friar Lawrence is most certainly correct, but after expounding his belief, the friar gets himself embroiled in all of the excess and passion he counsels against. The passion of the young lovers might be destructive, but it is also exquisitely beautiful; if Romeo and Juliet were moderate in their affection, their love would not strike such a chord.

Act III, scene 1

O, I am fortune's fool!

(See QUOTATIONS, *p. 62)*

Summary

As they walk in the street under the boiling sun, Benvolio suggests to Mercutio that they go indoors, fearing that a brawl will be unavoidable should they encounter Capulet men. Mercutio replies that Benvolio has as quick a temper as any man in Italy, and should not criticize others for their short fuses. Tybalt enters with a group of cronies. He approaches Benvolio and Mercutio and asks to speak with one of them. Annoyed, Mercutio begins to taunt and provoke him. Romeo enters. Tybalt turns his attention from Mercutio to Romeo, and calls Romeo a villain. Romeo, now secretly married to Juliet and thus Tybalt's kinsman, refuses to be angered by Tybalt's verbal attack. Tybalt commands Romeo to draw his sword. Romeo protests that he has good reason to love Tybalt, and does not wish to fight him. He asks that until Tybalt knows the reason for this love, he put aside his sword. Mercutio angrily draws his sword and declares with biting wit that if Romeo will not fight Tybalt, he will. Mercutio and Tybalt begin to fight. Romeo, attempting to restore peace, throws himself between the combatants. Tybalt stabs Mercutio under Romeo's arm, and as Mercutio falls, Tybalt and his men hurry away. Mercutio dies, cursing both the Montagues and the Capulets: "A plague o' both your houses" (III.i.87), and still pouring forth his wild witticisms: "Ask for me tomorrow, and / you shall find me a grave man" (III.i.93–94). Enraged, Romeo declares that his love for Juliet has made him effeminate, and that he should have fought Tybalt in Mercutio's place. When Tybalt, still angry, storms back onto the scene, Romeo draws his sword. They fight, and Romeo kills Tybalt. Benvolio urges Romeo to run; a group of citizens outraged at the recurring street fights is approaching. Romeo, shocked at what has happened, cries "O, I am fortune's fool!" and flees (III.i.131).

The Prince enters, accompanied by many citizens, and the Montagues and Capulets. Benvolio tells the Prince the story of the brawl, emphasizing Romeo's attempt to keep the peace, but Lady Capulet, Tybalt's aunt, cries that Benvolio is lying to protect the Montagues. She demands Romeo's life. Prince Escalus chooses instead to exile Romeo from Verona. He declares that should Romeo be found within the city, he will be killed.

Analysis

The sudden, fatal violence in the first scene of Act III, as well as the buildup to the fighting, serves as a reminder that, for all its emphasis on love, beauty, and romance, *Romeo and Juliet* still takes place in a masculine world in which notions of honor, pride, and status are prone to erupt in a fury of conflict. The viciousness and dangers of the play's social environment are dramatic tools that Shakespeare employs to make the lovers' romance seem even more precious and fragile—their relationship is the audience's only respite from the brutal world pressing against their love. The fights between Mercutio and Tybalt and then between Romeo and Tybalt are chaotic; Tybalt kills Mercutio under Romeo's arm, flees, and then suddenly, and inexplicably, returns to fight Romeo, who kills him in revenge. Passion outweighs reason at every turn.

Romeo's cry, "O, I am fortune's fool!" refers specifically to his unluckiness in being forced to kill his new wife's cousin, thereby getting himself banished (III.i.131). It also recalls the sense of fate that hangs over the play. Mercutio's response to his fate, however, is notable in the ways it diverges from Romeo's response. Romeo blames fate, or fortune, for what has happened to him. Mercutio curses the Montagues and Capulets. He seems to see people as the cause of his death, and gives no credit to any larger force.

Elizabethan society generally believed that a man too much in love lost his manliness. Romeo clearly subscribes to that belief, as can be seen when he states that his love for Juliet had made him "effeminate." Once again, however, this statement can be seen as a battle between the private world of love and the public world of honor, duty, and friendship. The Romeo who duels with Tybalt is the Romeo who Mercutio would call the "true" Romeo. The Romeo who sought to avoid confrontation out of concern for his wife is the person Juliet would recognize as her loving Romeo. The word *effeminate* is applied by the public world of honor upon those things it does not respect. In using the term to describe his present state, Romeo accepts the responsibilities thrust upon him by the social institutions of honor and family duty.

The arrival of the Prince and the angry citizens shifts the focus of the play to a different sort of public sphere. Romeo's killing of Tybalt is marked by rashness and vengeance, characteristics prized by noblemen, but which threaten the public order that citizens desire and the Prince has a responsibility to uphold. As one who has displayed such traits, Romeo is banished from Verona. Earlier, the Prince acted to repress the hatred of the Montagues and the Capulets in order to preserve public peace; now, still acting to avert outbreaks of violence, the Prince unwittingly acts to thwart the love of Romeo and Juliet. Consequently, with their love censured not only by the Montagues and Capulets but by the ruler of Verona, Romeo and Juliet's relationship puts Romeo in danger of violent reprisal from both from Juliet's kinsmen and the state.

Act III, scenes ii–iv

Summary: Act III, scene ii

In Capulet's house, Juliet longs for night to fall so that Romeo will come to her "untalked of and unseen" (III.ii.7). Suddenly the Nurse rushes in with news of the fight between Romeo and Tybalt. But the Nurse is so distraught, she stumbles over the words, making it sound as if Romeo is dead. Juliet assumes Romeo has killed himself, and she resigns to die herself. The Nurse then begins to moan about Tybalt's death, and Juliet briefly fears that both Romeo and Tybalt are dead. When the story is at last straight and Juliet understands that Romeo has killed Tybalt and been sentenced to exile, she curses nature that it should put "the spirit of a fiend" in Romeo's "sweet flesh" (III.ii.81–82). The Nurse echoes Juliet and curses Romeo's name, but Juliet denounces her for criticizing her husband, and adds that she regrets faulting him herself. Juliet claims that Romeo's banishment is worse than ten thousand slain Tybalts. She laments that she will die without a wedding night, a maiden-widow. The Nurse assures her, however, that she knows where Romeo is hiding, and will see to it that Romeo comes to her for their wedding night. Juliet gives the Nurse a ring to give to Romeo as a token of her love.

SUMMARY: ACT III, SCENE III

In Friar Lawrence's cell, Romeo is overcome with grief, and wonders what sentence the Prince has decreed. Friar Lawrence tells him he is lucky: the Prince has only banished him. Romeo claims that banishment is a penalty far worse than death, since he will have to live, but without Juliet. The friar tries to counsel Romeo but the youth is so unhappy that he will have none of it. Romeo falls to the floor. The Nurse arrives, and Romeo desperately asks her for news of Juliet. He assumes that Juliet now thinks of him as a murderer and threatens to stab himself. Friar Lawrence stops him and scolds him for being unmanly. He explains that Romeo has much to be grateful for: he and Juliet are both alive, and after matters have calmed down, Prince Escalus might change his mind. The friar sets forth a plan: Romeo will visit Juliet that night, but make sure to leave her chamber, and Verona, before the morning. He will then reside in Mantua until news of their marriage can be spread. The Nurse hands Romeo the ring from Juliet, and this physical symbol of their love revives his spirits. The Nurse departs, and Romeo bids Friar Lawrence farewell. He must prepare to visit Juliet and then flee to Mantua.

SUMMARY: ACT III, SCENE IV

Capulet, Lady Capulet, and Paris walk together. Capulet says that because of the terrible recent events, he has had no time to ask his daughter about her feelings for Paris. Lady Capulet states that she will know her daughter's thoughts by the morning. Paris is about to leave when Capulet calls him back and makes what he calls "a desperate tender of my child's love" (III.iv.12–13). Capulet says he thinks his daughter will listen to him, then corrects himself and states that he is sure Juliet will abide by his decision. He promises Paris that the wedding will be held on Wednesday, then stops suddenly and asks what day it is. Paris responds that it is Monday;

Capulet decides that Wednesday is too soon, and that the wedding should instead be held on Thursday.

Analysis: Act III, scenes ii–iv

The love between Romeo and Juliet, blissful in Act II, is tested under dire circumstances as the conflict between their families takes a turn more disastrous than either could have imagined. The respective manners in which the young lovers respond to their imminent separation helps define the essential qualities of their respective characters. After hearing that he is to be exiled, Romeo acts with customary drama: he is grief-stricken and overcome by his passion. He collapses on the floor. Romeo refuses to listen to reason and threatens to kill himself. Juliet, on the other hand, displays significant progress in her development from the simple, innocent girl of the first act to the brave, mature, and loyal woman of the play's conclusion. After criticizing Romeo for his role in Tybalt's death, and hearing the Nurse malign Romeo's name, Juliet regains control of herself and realizes that her loyalty must be to her husband rather than to Tybalt, her cousin.

Shakespeare creates an interesting psychological tension in *Romeo and Juliet* by consistently linking the intensity of young love with a suicidal impulse. Though love is generally the opposite of hatred, violence, and death, Shakespeare portrays self-annihilation as seemingly the only response to the overwhelming emotional experience that being young and in love constitutes. Romeo and Juliet seem to flirt with the idea of death throughout much of the play, and the possibility of suicide recurs often, foreshadowing the eventual deaths of the lovers in Act V. When Juliet misunderstands the Nurse and thinks that Romeo is dead, she does not think that he was killed, but that he killed himself. And thinking that Romeo is dead, Juliet quickly decides that she too must die. Her love for Romeo will allow no other course of action.

Romeo's actual threat of suicide in Friar Lawrence's cell, in which he desires to "sack / The hateful mansion" (III.iii.106–107) that is his body so that he may eradicate his name, recalls the balcony scene, in which Romeo scorns his Montague name in front of Juliet by saying, "Had I it written, I would tear the word" (II.i.99). In the balcony scene, a name seemed to be a simple thing that he could hold up in front of him and tear. Once torn, he could easily live without it. Now, with a better understanding of how difficult it is to escape the responsibilities and claims of family loyalty, of being a Montague, Romeo modifies his metaphor. No longer does he conceive of himself as able to tear his name. Instead, now he must rip it from his body, and, in the process, die.

Capulet's reasons for moving up the date of Juliet's marriage to Paris are not altogether clear. In later scenes, he states that he desires to bring some joy into a sad time, and to want to cure Juliet of her deep mourning (of course, ironically, she mourns her husband's banishment and not Tybalt's death). But it is also possible that in this escalating time of strife with the Montagues, Capulet wants all the political help he can get. A marriage between his daughter and Paris, a close kinsman to the Prince, would go a long way in this regard. Regardless of Capulet's motivation, his decision makes obvious the powerlessness of women in Verona. Juliet's impotence in this situation is driven home by the irony of Capulet's determination to push the wedding from Wednesday to Thursday when a few days earlier he wanted to postpone the wedding by two years.

ACT III, SCENE V

SUMMARY

Just before dawn, Romeo prepares to lower himself from Juliet's window to begin his exile. Juliet tries to convince Romeo that the birdcalls they hear are from the nightingale, a night bird, rather than from the lark, a morning bird. Romeo cannot entertain her claims; he must leave before the morning comes or be put to death. Juliet declares that the light outside comes not from the sun, but from some meteor. Overcome by love, Romeo responds that he will stay with Juliet, and that he does not care whether the Prince's men kill him. Faced with this turnaround, Juliet declares that the bird they heard was the lark; that it is dawn and he must flee. The Nurse enters to warn Juliet that Lady Capulet is approaching. Romeo and Juliet tearfully part. Romeo climbs out the window. Standing in the orchard below her window, Romeo promises Juliet that they will see one another again, but Juliet responds that he appears pale, as one dead in the bottom of a tomb. Romeo answers that, to him, she appears the same way, and that it is only sorrow that makes them both look pale. Romeo hurries away as Juliet pulls in the ladder and begs fate to bring him back to her quickly.

Lady Capulet calls to her daughter. Juliet wonders why her mother would come to speak to her so early in the morning. Unaware that her daughter is married to Romeo, Lady Capulet enters the room and mistakes Juliet's tears as continued grief for Tybalt. Lady Capulet tells Juliet of her deep desire to see "the villain Romeo" dead (III.v.80). In a complicated bit of punning every bit as impressive as the sexual punning of Mercutio and Romeo, Juliet leads her mother to believe that she also wishes Romeo's death, when in fact she is firmly stating her love for him. Lady Capulet tells Juliet about Capulet's plan for her to marry Paris on Thursday, explaining that he wishes to make her happy. Juliet is appalled. She rejects the match, saying "I will not marry yet; and when I do, I swear / It shall be Romeo—whom you know I hate— / Rather than Paris" (III.v.121–123). Capulet enters the chamber. When he learns of Juliet's determination to defy him he becomes enraged and threatens to disown Juliet if she refuses to obey him. When Juliet entreats her mother to intercede, her mother denies her help.

After Capulet and Lady Capulet storm away, Juliet asks her nurse how she might escape her predicament. The Nurse advises her to go through with the marriage to Paris—he is a better match, she says, and Romeo is as good as dead anyhow. Though disgusted by her nurse's disloyalty, Juliet pretends to agree, and tells her nurse that she is going to make confession at Friar Lawrence's. Juliet hurries to the friar, vowing that she will never again trust the Nurse's counsel. If the friar is unable to help her, Juliet comments to herself, she still has the power to take her own life.

Analysis

To combat the coming of the light, Juliet attempts once more to change the world through language: she claims the lark is truly a nightingale. Where in the balcony scene Romeo saw Juliet as transforming the night into day, here she is able to transform the day into the night. But just as their vows to throw off their names did not succeed in overcoming the social institutions that have plagued them, they cannot change time. As fits their characters, it is the more pragmatic Juliet who realizes that Romeo must leave; he is willing to die simply to remain by her side.

In a moment reminiscent of the balcony scene, once outside, Romeo bids farewell to Juliet as she stands at her window. Here, the lovers experience visions that blatantly foreshadow the end of the play. This is to be the last moment they spend alive in each other's company. When Juliet next sees Romeo he will be dead, and as she looks out of her window she seems to see him dead already: "O God, I have an ill-divining soul! / Methinks I see thee, now thou art so low, / As one dead in the bottom of a tomb. / Either my eyesight fails, or thou look'st pale" (III.v.54–57).

In the confrontation with her parents after Romeo's departure, Juliet shows her full maturity. She dominates the conversation with her mother, who cannot keep up with Juliet's intelligence and therefore has no idea that Juliet is proclaiming her love for Romeo under the guise of saying just the opposite. Her decision to break from the counsel of her disloyal nurse—and in fact to exclude her nurse from any part in her future actions—is another step in her development. Having a nurse is a mark of childhood; by abandoning her nurse and upholding her loyalty toward her husband, Juliet steps fully out of girlhood and into womanhood.

Shakespeare situates this maturation directly after Juliet's wedding night, linking the idea of development from childhood to adulthood with sexual experience. Indeed, Juliet feels so strong that she defies her father, but in that action she learns the limit of her power. Strong as she might be, Juliet is still a woman in a male-dominated world. One might think that Juliet should just take her father up on his offer to disown her and go to live with Romeo in Mantua. That is not an option. Juliet, as a woman, cannot leave society; and her father has the right to make her do as he wishes. Though defeated by her father, Juliet does not revert to being a little girl. She recognizes the limits of her power and, if another way cannot be found, determines to use it: for a woman in Verona who cannot control the direction of her life, suicide, the brute ability to live or not live that life, can represent the only means of asserting authority over the self.

Act IV, scenes i–ii

Summary: Act IV, scene i

In his cell, Friar Lawrence speaks with Paris about the latter's impending marriage to Juliet. Paris says that Juliet's grief about Tybalt's death has made her unbalanced, and that Capulet, in his wisdom, has determined they should marry soon so that Juliet can stop crying and put an end to her period of mourning. The friar remarks to himself that he wishes he were unaware of the reason that Paris' marriage to Juliet should be delayed.

Juliet enters, and Paris speaks to her lovingly, if somewhat arrogantly. Juliet responds indifferently, showing neither affection nor dislike. She remarks that she has not married him yet. On the pretense that he must hear Juliet's confession, Friar Lawrence ushers

Paris away, though not before Paris kisses Juliet once. After Paris leaves, Juliet asks Friar Lawrence for help, brandishing a knife and saying that she will kill herself rather than marry Paris. The friar proposes a plan: Juliet must consent to marry Paris; then, on the night before the wedding, she must drink a sleeping potion that will make her appear to be dead; she will be laid to rest in the Capulet tomb, and the friar will send word to Romeo in Mantua to help him retrieve her when she wakes up. She will then return to Mantua with Romeo, and be free to live with him away from their parents' hatred. Juliet consents to the plan wholeheartedly. Friar Lawrence gives her the sleeping potion.

Summary: Act IV, scene ii

Juliet returns home, where she finds Capulet and Lady Capulet preparing for the wedding. She surprises her parents by repenting her disobedience and cheerfully agreeing to marry Paris. Capulet is so pleased that he insists on moving the marriage up a day, to Wednesday—tomorrow. Juliet heads to her chambers to, ostensibly, prepare for her wedding. Capulet heads off to tell Paris the news.

Analysis: Act IV, scenes i–ii

Friar Lawrence is the wiliest and most scheming character in *Romeo and Juliet*: he secretly marries the two lovers, spirits Romeo to Mantua, and stages Juliet's death. The friar's machinations seem also to be tools of fate. Yet despite the role Friar Lawrence plays in bringing about the lovers' deaths, Shakespeare never presents him in a negative, or even ambiguous, light. He is always treated as a benign, wise presence. The tragic failure of his plans is treated as a disastrous accident for which Friar Lawrence bears no responsibility.

In contrast, it is a challenge to situate Paris along the play's moral continuum. He is not exactly an adversary to Romeo and Juliet, since he never acts consciously to harm them or go against their wishes. Like almost everyone else, he knows nothing of their relationship. Paris's feelings for Juliet are also a subject of some ambiguity, since the audience is never allowed access to his thoughts. Later textual evidence does indicate that Paris harbors a legitimate love for Juliet, and though he arrogantly assumes Juliet will want to marry him, Paris never treats her unkindly. Nevertheless, because she does not love him, he represents a real and frightening potentiality for Juliet.

Act IV, scenes iii–iv

Summary: Act IV, scene iii

In her bedchamber, Juliet asks the Nurse to let her spend the night by herself, and repeats the request to Lady Capulet when she arrives. Alone, clutching the vial given to her by Friar Lawrence, she wonders what will happen when she drinks it. If the friar is untrustworthy and seeks merely to hide his role in her marriage to Romeo, she might die; or, if Romeo is late for some reason, she might awaken in the tomb and go mad with fear. She has a vision in which she sees Tybalt's ghost searching for Romeo. She begs Tybalt's ghost to quit its search for Romeo, and toasting to Romeo, drinks the contents of the vial.

Summary: Act IV, scene iv

Early the next morning, the Capulet house is aflutter with preparations for the wedding. Capulet sends the Nurse to go wake Juliet. She finds Juliet dead and begins to wail, soon joined by both Lady Capulet and Capulet. Paris arrives with Friar Lawrence and a group of musicians for the wedding. When he learns what has happened, Paris joins in the lamentations. The friar reminds them all that Juliet has gone to a better place, and urges them to make ready for her funeral. Sorrowfully, they comply, and exit.

Left behind, the musicians begin to pack up, their task cut short. Peter, the Capulet servant, enters and asks the musicians to play a happy tune to ease his sorrowful heart. The musicians refuse, arguing that to play such music would be inappropriate. Angered, Peter insults the musicians, who respond in kind. After singing a final insult at the musicians, Peter leaves. The musicians decide to wait for the mourners to return so that they might get to eat the lunch that will be served.

Analysis: Act IV, scenes iii–iv

Once again Juliet demonstrates her strength. She comes up with reason after reason why drinking the sleeping potion might cause her harm, physical or psychological, but chooses to drink it anyway. In this action she not only attempts to circumvent the forces that obstruct her relationship with Romeo, she takes full responsibility for herself. She recognizes that drinking the potion might lead her to madness or to death. Drinking the potion therefore constitutes an action in which she takes her life into her own hands, and determines its worth to her. In addition to the obvious foreshadow in Juliet's vision of Tybalt's vengeful ghost, her drinking of the potion also hints at future events. She drinks the potion just as Romeo will later drink the Apothecary's poison. In drinking the potion she not only demonstrates a willingness to take her life into her own hands, she goes against what is expected of women and takes action.

In their mourning for Juliet, the Capulets appear less as a hostile force arrayed against the lovers and more as individuals. The audience gains an understanding of the immense hopes that the Capulets had placed in Juliet, as well as a sense of their love for her. Similarly, Paris's love for Juliet seems wholly legitimate. His wailing cannot simply be taken as grief over the loss of a wife who might have brought him fortune. It seems more personal than that, more like grief over the loss of a loved one.

Many productions of *Romeo and Juliet* cut the scene depicting Peter and the musicians. Productions do this for good reason: the scene's humor and traded insults seem ill placed at such a tragic moment in the play. If one looks at the scene as merely comic relief, it is possible to argue that it acts as a sort of caesura, a moment for the audience to catch its breath from the tragedy of Act IV before heading into the even greater tragedy of Act V. If one looks at the scene in context with the earlier scenes that include servants a second argument can be made for why Shakespeare included it. From each scene including servants, we gain a unique perspective of the events going on in the play. Here, in the figure of the musicians, we get a profoundly different view of the reaction of the lower classes to the tragedy of Juliet's death. Initially the musicians are wary about playing a happy song because it will be considered improper, no matter their explanations. It is not, after all, for a mere musician to give explanations to mourning noblemen. As the scene progresses it becomes clear that the musicians do not really care much about Juliet or the tragedy in which she is involved. They care more about the fact that they are out of a job, and perhaps, that they will miss out on a free lunch. In other words, this great tragedy, which is, undoubtedly, a tragedy of epic proportions, is still not a tragedy to everyone.

Act V, scenes i–ii

Summary: Act V, scene i

Then I defy you, stars.

(*See* QUOTATIONS, *p.* 62)

On Wednesday morning, on a street in Mantua, a cheerful Romeo describes a wonderful dream he had the night before: Juliet found him lying dead, but she kissed him, and breathed new life into his body. Just then, Balthasar enters, and Romeo greets him happily, saying that Balthasar must have come from Verona with news of Juliet and his father. Romeo comments that nothing can be ill in the world if Juliet is well. Balthasar replies that nothing can be ill, then, for Juliet is well: she is in heaven, found dead that morning at her home. Thunderstruck, Romeo cries out "Then I defy you, stars" (V.i.24).

He tells Balthasar to get him pen and paper (with which he writes a letter for Balthasar to give to Montague) and to hire horses, and says that he will return to Verona that night. Balthasar says that Romeo seems so distraught that he is afraid to leave him, but Romeo insists. Romeo suddenly stops and asks if Balthasar is carrying a letter from Friar Lawrence. Balthasar says he is not, and Romeo sends his servant on his way. Once Balthasar is gone, Romeo says that he will lie with Juliet that night. He goes to find an apothecary, a seller of drugs. After telling the man in the shop that he looks poor, Romeo offers to pay him well for a vial of poison. The Apothecary says that he has just such a thing, but that selling poison in Mantua carries the death sentence. Romeo replies that the Apothecary is too poor to refuse the sale. The Apothecary finally relents and sells Romeo the poison. Once alone, Romeo speaks to the vial, declaring that he will go to Juliet's tomb and kill himself.

Summary: Act V, scene ii

At his cell, Friar Lawrence speaks with Friar John, whom he had earlier sent to Mantua with a letter for Romeo. He asks John how Romeo responded to his letter (which described the plan involving Juliet's false death). Friar John replies that he was unable to deliver the letter because he was shut up in a quarantined house due to an outbreak of plague. Friar Lawrence becomes upset, realizing that if Romeo does not know about Juliet's false death, there will be no one to retrieve her from the tomb when she awakes. (He does not know that Romeo has learned of Juliet's death and believes it to be real.)

Sending for a crowbar, Friar Lawrence declares that he will have to rescue Juliet from the tomb on his own. He sends another letter to Romeo to warn him about what has happened, and plans to keep Juliet in his cell until Romeo arrives.

ANALYSIS: ACT V, SCENES I–II

The sequence of near misses in this section reveals the inescapable work of fate. There is no reason for the friar's plan to go wrong. But an outbreak of plague forces Friar John into quarantine and prevents him from delivering Friar Lawrence's letter to Romeo, while Balthasar seeks out Romeo with news of Juliet's death. Just as the audience senses an inviolable fate descending on Romeo, so too does Romeo feel himself trapped by fate. But the fate the audience recognizes and the fate Romeo sees as surrounding him are very different. The audience knows that both Romeo and Juliet are bound to die; Romeo knows only that fate has somehow tried to separate him from Juliet. When Romeo screams "Then I defy you, stars" he is screaming against the fate that he believes is thwarting his desires (V.i.24). He attempts to defy that fate by killing himself and spending eternity with Juliet: "Well, Juliet," he says, "I will lie with thee tonight" (V.i.34). Tragically, it is Romeo's very decision to avoid his destiny that actually brings fate about. In killing himself over the sleeping Juliet he ensures their ultimate double suicide.

Through the irony of Romeo's defiance rebounding upon himself, Shakespeare demonstrates the extreme power of fate: nothing can stand in its way. All factors swing in its favor: the outbreak of the plague, Balthasar's transmission of the message of Juliet's death, and Capulet's decision to move Juliet's wedding date. But fate is also something attached to the social institutions of the world in which Romeo and Juliet live. This destiny, brought about by the interplay of societal norms from which Romeo and Juliet cannot escape, seems equally powerful, though less divine. It is a fate created by man, and man's inability to see through the absurdity of the world he has created. Now, in this scene, we see Romeo as agent of his own fate. The fortune that befalls Romeo and Juliet is internal rather than external. It is determined by the natures and choices of its two protagonists. Were Romeo not so rash and emotional, so quick to fall into melancholy, the double suicide would not have occurred. Had Juliet felt it possible to explain the truth to her parents, the double suicide might not have occurred. But to wish someone were not as they were is to wish for the impossible. The love between

Romeo and Juliet exists precisely because they are who they are. The destructive, suicidal nature of their love is just as much an aspect of their natures, as individuals and couple.

In the character of the Apothecary, once again, Shakespeare provides a secondary example of the paradoxical and pressing social forces at work in the play. The Apothecary does not wish to sell poison because it is illegal, banned by society. But it is the same society that makes him poor, and which insists on validity of the differences between rich and poor. The Apothecary is pushed to sell the poison by external forces that he, like Romeo, feels completely unable to control.

Act V, scene III

Summary

In the churchyard that night, Paris enters with a torch-bearing servant. He orders the page to withdraw, then begins scattering flowers on Juliet's grave. He hears a whistle—the servant's warning that someone is approaching. He withdraws into the darkness. Romeo, carrying a crowbar, enters with Balthasar. He tells Balthasar that he has come to open the Capulet tomb in order to take back a valuable ring he had given to Juliet. Then he orders Balthasar to leave, and, in the morning, to deliver to Montague the letter Romeo had given him. Balthasar withdraws, but, mistrusting his master's intentions, lingers to watch.

From his hiding place, Paris recognizes Romeo as the man who murdered Tybalt, and thus as the man who indirectly murdered Juliet, since it is her grief for her cousin that is supposed to have killed her. As Romeo has been exiled from the city on penalty of death, Paris thinks that Romeo must hate the Capulets so much that he has returned to the tomb to do some dishonor to the corpse of either Tybalt or Juliet. In a rage, Paris accosts Romeo. Romeo pleads with him to leave, but Paris refuses. They draw their swords and fight. Paris's page runs off to get the civil watch. Romeo kills Paris. As he dies, Paris asks to be laid near Juliet in the tomb, and Romeo consents.

Romeo descends into the tomb carrying Paris's body. He finds Juliet lying peacefully, and wonders how she can still look so beautiful—as if she were not dead at all. Romeo speaks to Juliet of his intention to spend eternity with her, describing himself as shaking "the yoke of inauspicious stars / From this world-wearied flesh"

(V.iii.111–112). He kisses Juliet, drinks the poison, kisses Juliet again, and dies.

Just then, Friar Lawrence enters the churchyard. He encounters Balthasar, who tells him that Romeo is in the tomb. Balthasar says that he fell asleep and dreamed that Romeo fought with and killed someone. Troubled, the friar enters the tomb, where he finds Paris's body and then Romeo's. As the friar takes in the bloody scene, Juliet wakes.

Juliet asks the friar where her husband is. Hearing a noise that he believes is the coming of the watch, the friar quickly replies that both Romeo and Paris are dead, and that she must leave with him. Juliet refuses to leave, and the friar, fearful that the watch is imminent, exits without her. Juliet sees Romeo dead beside her, and surmises from the empty vial that he has drunk poison. Hoping she might die by the same poison, Juliet kisses his lips, but to no avail. Hearing the approaching watch, Juliet unsheathes Romeo's dagger and, saying, "O happy dagger, / This is thy sheath," stabs herself (V.iii.171). She dies upon Romeo's body.

Chaos reigns in the churchyard, where Paris's page has brought the watch. The watchmen discover bloodstains near the tomb; they hold Balthasar and Friar Lawrence, who they discovered loitering nearby. The Prince and the Capulets enter. Romeo, Juliet, and Paris are discovered in the tomb. Montague arrives, declaring that Lady Montague has died of grief for Romeo's exile. The Prince shows Montague his son's body. Upon the Prince's request, Friar Lawrence succinctly tells the story of Romeo and Juliet's secret marriage and its consequences. Balthasar gives the Prince the letter Romeo had previously written to his father. The Prince says that it confirms the friar's story. He scolds the Capulets and Montagues, calling the tragedy a consequence of their feud and reminding them that he himself has lost two close kinsmen: Mercutio and Paris. Capulet and Montague clasp hands and agree to put their vendetta behind them. Montague says that he will build a golden statue of Juliet, and Capulet insists that he will raise Romeo's likeness in gold beside hers. The Prince takes the group away to discuss these events, pronouncing that there has never been "a story of more woe / Than this of Juliet and her Romeo" (V.iii.309).

ANALYSIS

The deaths of Romeo and Juliet occur in a sequence of compounding stages: first, Juliet drinks a potion that makes her *appear* dead.

Thinking her dead, Romeo then drinks a poison that *actually* kills him. Seeing him dead, Juliet stabs herself through the heart with a dagger. Their parallel consumption of mysterious potions lends their deaths a peaceful symmetry, which is broken by Juliet's dramatic dagger stroke. Throughout *Romeo and Juliet,* Shakespeare has held up the possibility of suicide as an inherent aspect of intense love. Passion cannot be stifled, and when combined with the vigor of youth, it expresses itself through the most convenient outlet. Romeo and Juliet long to live for love or die for it. Shakespeare considers this suicidal impulse not as something separate from love, but rather as an element as much a part of it as the romantic euphoria of Act II. As such, the double suicide represents both the fulfillment of their love for each other and the self-destructive impulse that has surged and flexed beneath their love for the duration of the play. The Friar's embodiment of good and evil are united in a single act: suicide. Juliet tries to kill herself with a kiss: an act of love as intended violence. When that fails she stabs herself with a "happy dagger," "happy" because it reunites her with her love (V.iii.168). Violence becomes an assertion of autonomy over the self and a final deed of profound love.

Social and private forces converge in the suicides of Romeo and Juliet. Paris, Juliet's would-be husband, challenges Romeo, her actual husband, pitting the embodiments of Juliet's lack of power in the public sphere against her very real ability to give her heart where she wishes. Through the arrival of the Prince, the law imposes itself, seeking to restore the peace in the name of social order and government. Montague and Capulet arrive, rehashing family tension. None of these forces are able to exert any influence on the young lovers. We have seen Romeo and Juliet time and again attempt to reconfigure the world through language so that their love might have a place to exist peacefully. That language, though powerful in the moment, could never counter the vast forces of the social world. Through suicide, the lovers are able not just to escape the world that oppresses them. Further, in the final blazing glory of their deaths, they transfigure that world. The feud between their families ends. Prince Escalus—the law—recognizes the honor and value due the lovers. In dying, love has conquered all, its passion is shown to be the brightest, most powerful. It seems at last that Friar Lawrence's words have come to be: "These violent delights have violent ends / And in their triumph die" (II.v.9–10). The extremely intense passion of Romeo and Juliet has trumped all other passions, and in coming to its violent end has forced those other passions, also, to cease.

One senses the grand irony that in death Romeo and Juliet have created the world that would have allowed their love to live. That irony does exist, and it is tragic. But because of the power and beauty of their love, it is hard to see Romeo and Juliet's death as a simple tragedy. Romeo and Juliet's deaths are tragic, but this tragedy was fated: by the stars, by the violent world in which they live, by the play, and by their very natures. We, as an audience, *want* this death, this tragedy. At the play's end, we do not feel sad for the loss of life as much as we feel wrenched by the incredible act of love that Romeo and Juliet have committed as monuments to each other and their love. Romeo and Juliet have been immortalized as the archetypes of true love not because their tragic deaths bury their parents' strife, but rather because they are willing to sacrifice everything—including themselves—for their love. That Romeo and Juliet must kill themselves to preserve their love is tragic. That they do kill themselves to preserve their love makes them transcendent.

Important Quotations Explained

1. But soft, what light through yonder window breaks?
It is the east, and Juliet is the sun.
Arise, fair sun, and kill the envious moon,
Who is already sick and pale with grief
That thou, her maid, art far more fair than she. . . .
The brightness of her cheek would shame those stars
As daylight doth a lamp; her eye in heaven
Would through the airy region stream so bright
That birds would sing and think it were not night.

Romeo speaks these lines in the so-called balcony scene, when, hiding in the Capulet orchard after the feast, he sees Juliet leaning out of a high window (II.i.44–64). Though it is late at night, Juliet's surpassing beauty makes Romeo imagine that she is the sun, transforming the darkness into daylight. Romeo likewise personifies the moon, calling it "sick and pale with grief" at the fact that Juliet, the sun, is far brighter and more beautiful. Romeo then compares Juliet to the stars, claiming that she eclipses the stars as daylight overpowers a lamp—her eyes alone shine so bright that they will convince the birds to sing at night as if it were day.

This quote is important because in addition to initiating one of the play's most beautiful and famous sequences of poetry, it is a prime example of the light/dark motif that runs throughout the play. Many scenes in *Romeo and Juliet* are set either late at night or early in the morning, and Shakespeare often uses the contrast between night and day to explore opposing alternatives in a given situation. Here, Romeo imagines Juliet transforming darkness into light; later, after their wedding night, Juliet convinces Romeo momentarily that the daylight is actually night (so that he doesn't yet have to leave her room).

2. O Romeo, Romeo,
wherefore art thou Romeo?
Deny thy father and refuse thy name,
Or if thou wilt not, be but sworn my love,
And I'll no longer be a Capulet.

Juliet speaks these lines, perhaps the most famous in the play, in the balcony scene (II.i.74–78). Leaning out of her upstairs window, unaware that Romeo is below in the orchard, she asks why Romeo must be Romeo—why he must be a Montague, the son of her family's greatest enemy ("wherefore" means "why," not "where"; Juliet is not, as is often assumed, asking where Romeo is). Still unaware of Romeo's presence, she asks him to deny his family for her love. She adds, however, that if he will not, she will deny her family in order to be with him if he merely tells her that he loves her.

A major theme in *Romeo and Juliet* is the tension between social and family identity (represented by one's name) and one's inner identity. Juliet believes that love stems from one's inner identity, and that the feud between the Montagues and the Capulets is a product of the outer identity, based only on names. She thinks of Romeo in individual terms, and thus her love for him overrides her family's hatred for the Montague name. She says that if Romeo were not called "Romeo" or "Montague," he would still be the person she loves. "What's in a name?" she asks. "That which we call a rose / By any other word would smell as sweet" (II.i.85–86).

3. O, then I see Queen Mab hath been with you. . . .
She is the fairies' midwife, and she comes
In shape no bigger than an agate stone
On the forefinger of an alderman,
Drawn with a team of little atomi
Athwart men's noses as they lie asleep.

Mercutio's famous Queen Mab speech is important for the stunning quality of its poetry and for what it reveals about Mercutio's character, but it also has some interesting thematic implications (I.iv.53–59). Mercutio is trying to convince Romeo to set aside his lovesick melancholy over Rosaline and come along to the Capulet feast. When Romeo says that he is depressed because of a dream, Mercutio launches on a lengthy, playful description of Queen Mab, the fairy who supposedly brings dreams to sleeping humans. The main point of the passage is that the dreams Queen Mab brings are directly related to the person who dreams them—lovers dream of love, soldiers of war, etc. But in the process of making this rather prosaic point Mercutio falls into a sort of wild bitterness in which he seems to see dreams as destructive and delusional.

4. From forth the fatal loins of these two foes
A pair of star-crossed lovers take their life,
Whose misadventured piteous overthrows
Doth with their death bury their parents' strife. . . .

O, I am fortune's fool! . . .

Then I defy you, stars.

This trio of quotes advances the theme of fate as it plays out through the story: the first is spoken by the Chorus (Prologue.5–8), the second by Romeo after he kills Tybalt (III.i.131), and the third by Romeo upon learning of Juliet's death (V.i.24). The Chorus's remark that Romeo and Juliet are "star-crossed" and fated to "take their li[ves]" informs the audience that the lovers are destined to die tragically. Romeo's remark "O, I am fortune's fool!" illustrates the fact that Romeo sees himself as subject to the whims of fate. When he cries out "Then I defy you, stars," after learning of Juliet's death, he declares himself openly opposed to the destiny that so grieves him. Sadly, in "defying" fate he actually brings it about. Romeo's suicide prompts Juliet to kill herself, thereby ironically fulfilling the lovers' tragic destiny.

Key Facts

FULL TITLE

The Most Excellent and Lamentable Tragedy of Romeo and Juliet

AUTHOR

William Shakespeare

TYPE OF WORK

Play

GENRE

Tragic drama

LANGUAGE

English

TIME AND PLACE WRITTEN

London, mid-1590s

DATE OF FIRST PUBLICATION

1597 (in the First Quarto, which was likely an unauthorized incomplete edition); 1599 (in the Second Quarto, which was authorized)

PUBLISHER

Thomas Creede (in the Second Quarto, using the title *The Most Excellent and Lamentable Tragedie, of Romeo and Juliet*)

CLIMAX

The deaths of Romeo and Juliet in the Capulet tomb (V.iii)

PROTAGONISTS

Romeo; Juliet

ANTAGONISTS

The feuding Montagues and Capulets; Tybalt; the Prince and citizens of Verona; fate

SETTINGS (TIME)

Renaissance (fourteenth or fifteenth century)

SETTINGS (PLACE)

Verona and Mantua (cities in northern Italy)

POINT OF VIEW

Insofar as a play has a point of view, that of Romeo and Juliet; occasionally the play uses the point of view of the Montague and Capulet servants to illuminate the actions of their masters.

FALLING ACTION

The end of Act V, scene iii, when the Prince and the parents discover the bodies of Romeo and Juliet, and agree to put aside their feud in the interest of peace.

TENSE

Present

FORESHADOWING

The Chorus's first speech declaring that Romeo and Juliet are doomed to die and "star-crossed." The lovers' frequent thoughts of death: "My grave is like to be my wedding bed" (Juliet, I.v.132). The lovers' thoughts of suicide, as when Romeo threatens to kill himself after killing Tybalt. Friar Lawrence's warnings to behave moderately if Romeo and Juliet wish to avoid tragedy: "These violent delights have violent ends . . . Therefore love moderately" (II.v.9–14). The lovers' mutual impression that the other looks pale and deathlike after their wedding night (III.v). Juliet's faked death by Friar Lawrence's potion. Romeo's dream-vision of Juliet kissing his lips while he is dead (V.i). Romeo's outbursts against fate: "O, I am fortune's fool!" (III.i.131) and "Then I defy you, stars" (V.i.24).

TONES

Passionate, romantic, intense, rhapsodic, violent, prone to extremes of emotion (ecstasy, rage, misery, etc.)

THEMES

The forcefulness of love; love as a cause of violence; the individual versus society; the inevitability of fate

MOTIFS

Light/dark imagery; opposite points of view

SYMBOLS

Poison; thumb-biting; Queen Mab

Study Questions

1. *What effect does the accelerated time scheme have on the play's development? Is it plausible that a love story of this magnitude could take place so quickly? Does the play seem to take place over as little time as it actually occupies?*

Because of the intensity of the relationship between Romeo and Juliet and the complex development of events during the few days of the play's action, the story can certainly seem to take place over a time span much longer than the one it actually occupies. By compressing all the events of the love story into just a few days, Shakespeare adds weight to every moment, and gives the sense that the action is happening so quickly that characters barely have time to react, and, by the end, that matters are careening out of control. This rush heightens the sense of pressure that hangs in the atmosphere of the play. While it may not seem plausible for a story such as Romeo and Juliet to take place over a span of only four days in the real world, this abbreviated time scheme makes sense in the universe of the play.

2. *Compare and contrast the characters of Romeo and Juliet. How do they develop throughout the play? What makes them fall in love with one another?*

Romeo is a passionate, extreme, excitable, intelligent, and moody young man, well-liked and admired throughout Verona. He is loyal to his friends, but his behavior is somewhat unpredictable. At the beginning of the play, he mopes over his hopeless unrequited love for Rosaline. In Juliet, Romeo finds a legitimate object for the extraordinary passion that he is capable of feeling, and his unyielding love for her takes control of him.

Juliet, on the other hand, is an innocent girl, a child at the beginning of the play, and is startled by the sudden power of her love for Romeo. Guided by her feelings for him, she develops very quickly into a determined, capable, mature, and loyal woman who tempers her extreme feelings of love with sober-mindedness.

The attraction between Romeo and Juliet is immediate and overwhelming, and neither of the young lovers comments on or pretends to understand its cause. Each mentions the other's beauty, but it seems that destiny, rather than any particular character trait, has drawn them together. Their love for one another is so undeniable that neither they nor the audience feels the need to question or explain it.

3. *Compare and contrast the characters of Tybalt and Mercutio. Why does Mercutio hate Tybalt?*

As Mercutio tells Benvolio, he hates Tybalt for being a slave to fashion and vanity, one of "such antic, lisping, affecting phantas- / ims, these new tuners of accent! . . . these fashionmongers, these 'pardon-me's' " (II.iii.25–29). Mercutio is so insistent that the reader feels compelled to accept this description of Tybalt's character as definitive. Tybalt does prove Mercutio's words true: he demonstrates himself to be as witty, vain, and prone to violence as he is fashionable, easily insulted, and defensive. To the self-possessed Mercutio, Tybalt seems a caricature; to Tybalt, the brilliant, earthy, and unconventional Mercutio is probably incomprehensible. (It might be interesting to compare Mercutio's comments about Tybalt to Hamlet's description of the foppish Osric in Act V, scene ii of *Hamlet,* lines 140–146.)

How to Write Literary Analysis

The Literary Essay: A Step-by-Step Guide

When you read for pleasure, your only goal is enjoyment. You might find yourself reading to get caught up in an exciting story, to learn about an interesting time or place, or just to pass time. Maybe you're looking for inspiration, guidance, or a reflection of your own life. There are as many different, valid ways of reading a book as there are books in the world.

When you read a work of literature in an English class, however, you're being asked to read in a special way: you're being asked to perform *literary analysis*. To analyze something means to break it down into smaller parts and then examine how those parts work, both individually and together. Literary analysis involves examining all the parts of a novel, play, short story, or poem—elements such as character, setting, tone, and imagery—and thinking about how the author uses those elements to create certain effects.

A literary essay isn't a book review: you're not being asked whether or not you liked a book or whether you'd recommend it to another reader. A literary essay also isn't like the kind of book report you wrote when you were younger, where your teacher wanted you to summarize the book's action. A high school- or college-level literary essay asks, "How does this piece of literature actually work?" "How does it do what it does?" and, "Why might the author have made the choices he or she did?"

The Seven Steps

No one is born knowing how to analyze literature; it's a skill you learn and a process you can master. As you gain more practice with this kind of thinking and writing, you'll be able to craft a method that works best for you. But until then, here are seven basic steps to writing a well-constructed literary essay:

1. *Ask questions*
2. *Collect evidence*
3. *Construct a thesis*

4. *Develop and organize arguments*
5. *Write the introduction*
6. *Write the body paragraphs*
7. *Write the conclusion*

---

1. Ask Questions

When you're assigned a literary essay in class, your teacher will often provide you with a list of writing prompts. Lucky you! Now all you have to do is choose one. Do yourself a favor and pick a topic that interests you. You'll have a much better (not to mention easier) time if you start off with something you enjoy thinking about. If you are asked to come up with a topic by yourself, though, you might start to feel a little panicked. Maybe you have too many ideas—or none at all. Don't worry. Take a deep breath and start by asking yourself these questions:

- **What struck you?** Did a particular image, line, or scene linger in your mind for a long time? If it fascinated you, chances are you can draw on it to write a fascinating essay.
- **What confused you?** Maybe you were surprised to see a character act in a certain way, or maybe you didn't understand why the book ended the way it did. Confusing moments in a work of literature are like a loose thread in a sweater: if you pull on it, you can unravel the entire thing. Ask yourself why the author chose to write about that character or scene the way he or she did and you might tap into some important insights about the work as a whole.
- **Did you notice any patterns?** Is there a phrase that the main character uses constantly or an image that repeats throughout the book? If you can figure out how that pattern weaves through the work and what the significance of that pattern is, you've almost got your entire essay mapped out.
- **Did you notice any contradictions or ironies?** Great works of literature are complex; great literary essays recognize and explain those complexities. Maybe the title (*Happy Days*) totally disagrees with the book's subject matter (hungry orphans dying in the woods). Maybe the main character acts one way around his family and a completely different way around his friends and associates. If you can find a way to explain a work's contradictory elements, you've got the seeds of a great essay.

At this point, you don't need to know exactly what you're going to say about your topic; you just need a place to begin your exploration. You can help direct your reading and brainstorming by formulating your topic as a *question,* which you'll then try to answer in your essay. The best questions invite critical debates and discussions, not just a rehashing of the summary. Remember, you're looking for something you can *prove or argue* based on evidence you find in the text. Finally, remember to keep the scope of your question in mind: is this a topic you can adequately address within the word or page limit you've been given? Conversely, is this a topic big enough to fill the required length?

GOOD QUESTIONS

"Are Romeo and Juliet's parents responsible for the deaths of their children?"

"Why do pigs keep showing up in LORD OF THE FLIES*?"*

"Are Dr. Frankenstein and his monster alike? How?"

BAD QUESTIONS

"What happens to Scout in TO KILL A MOCKINGBIRD*?"*

"What do the other characters in JULIUS CAESAR *think about Caesar?"*

"How does Hester Prynne in THE SCARLET LETTER *remind me of my sister?"*

---

2. COLLECT EVIDENCE

Once you know what question you want to answer, it's time to scour the book for things that will help you answer the question. Don't worry if you don't know what you want to say yet—right now you're just collecting ideas and material and letting it all percolate. Keep track of passages, symbols, images, or scenes that deal with your topic. Eventually, you'll start making connections between these examples and your thesis will emerge.

Here's a brief summary of the various parts that compose each and every work of literature. These are the elements that you will analyze in your essay, and which you will offer as evidence to support your arguments. For more on the parts of literary works, see the Glossary of Literary Terms at the end of this section.

ELEMENTS OF STORY These are the *whats* of the work—what happens, where it happens, and to whom it happens.

- **Plot:** All of the events and actions of the work.
- **Character:** The people who act and are acted upon in a literary work. The main character of a work is known as the *protagonist*.
- **Conflict:** The central tension in the work. In most cases, the protagonist wants something, while opposing forces (antagonists) hinder the protagonist's progress.
- **Setting:** When and where the work takes place. Elements of setting include location, time period, time of day, weather, social atmosphere, and economic conditions.
- **Narrator:** The person telling the story. The narrator may straightforwardly report what happens, convey the subjective opinions and perceptions of one or more characters, or provide commentary and opinion in his or her own voice.
- **Themes:** The main idea or message of the work—usually an abstract idea about people, society, or life in general. A work may have many themes, which may be in tension with one another.

ELEMENTS OF STYLE These are the *hows*—how the characters speak, how the story is constructed, and how language is used throughout the work.

- **Structure and organization:** How the parts of the work are assembled. Some novels are narrated in a linear, chronological fashion, while others skip around in time. Some plays follow a traditional three- or five-act structure, while others are a series of loosely connected scenes. Some authors deliberately leave gaps in their works, leaving readers to puzzle out the missing information. A work's structure and organization can tell you a lot about the kind of message it wants to convey.
- **Point of view:** The perspective from which a story is told. In *first-person point of view,* the narrator involves him or herself in the story. ("I went to the store"; "We watched in horror as the bird slammed into the window.") A first-person narrator is usually the protagonist of the work, but not always. In *third-person point of view,* the narrator does not participate

in the story. A third-person narrator may closely follow a specific character, recounting that individual character's thoughts or experiences, or it may be what we call an *omniscient* narrator. Omniscient narrators see and know all: they can witness any event in any time or place and are privy to the inner thoughts and feelings of all characters. Remember that the narrator and the author are not the same thing!

- **Diction:** Word choice. Whether a character uses dry, clinical language or flowery prose with lots of exclamation points can tell you a lot about his or her attitude and personality.
- **Syntax:** Word order and sentence construction. Syntax is a crucial part of establishing an author's narrative voice. Ernest Hemingway, for example, is known for writing in very short, straightforward sentences, while James Joyce characteristically wrote in long, incredibly complicated lines.
- **Tone:** The mood or feeling of the text. Diction and syntax often contribute to the tone of a work. A novel written in short, clipped sentences that use small, simple words might feel brusque, cold, or matter-of-fact.
- **Imagery:** Language that appeals to the senses, representing things that can be seen, smelled, heard, tasted, or touched.
- **Figurative language:** Language that is not meant to be interpreted literally. The most common types of figurative language are *metaphors* and *similes,* which compare two unlike things in order to suggest a similarity between them—for example, "All the world's a stage," or "The moon is like a ball of green cheese." (Metaphors say one thing *is* another thing; similes claim that one thing is *like* another thing.)

---

3. Construct a Thesis

When you've examined all the evidence you've collected and know how you want to answer the question, it's time to write your thesis statement. A *thesis* is a claim about a work of literature that needs to be supported by evidence and arguments. The thesis statement is the heart of the literary essay, and the bulk of your paper will be spent trying to prove this claim. A good thesis will be:

- **Arguable.** "*The Great Gatsby* describes New York society in the 1920s" isn't a thesis—it's a fact.

- **Provable through textual evidence.** "*Hamlet* is a confusing but ultimately very well-written play" is a weak thesis because it offers the writer's personal opinion about the book. Yes, it's arguable, but it's not a claim that can be proved or supported with examples taken from the play itself.
- **Surprising.** "Both George and Lenny change a great deal in *Of Mice and Men*" is a weak thesis because it's obvious. A really strong thesis will argue for a reading of the text that is not immediately apparent.
- **Specific.** "Dr. Frankenstein's monster tells us a lot about the human condition" is *almost* a really great thesis statement, but it's still too vague. What does the writer mean by "a lot"? *How* does the monster tell us so much about the human condition?

Good Thesis Statements

Question: In *Romeo and Juliet*, which is more powerful in shaping the lovers' story: fate or foolishness?

Thesis: "Though Shakespeare defines Romeo and Juliet as 'star-crossed lovers' and images of stars and planets appear throughout the play, a closer examination of that celestial imagery reveals that the stars are merely witnesses to the characters' foolish activities and not the causes themselves."

Question: How does the bell jar function as a symbol in Sylvia Plath's *The Bell Jar*?

Thesis: "A bell jar is a bell-shaped glass that has three basic uses: to hold a specimen for observation, to contain gases, and to maintain a vacuum. The bell jar appears in each of these capacities in *The Bell Jar*, Plath's semi-autobiographical novel, and each appearance marks a different stage in Esther's mental breakdown."

Question: Would Piggy in *The Lord of the Flies* make a good island leader if he were given the chance?

Thesis: "Though the intelligent, rational, and innovative Piggy has the mental characteristics of a good leader, he ultimately lacks the social skills necessary to be an effective one. Golding emphasizes this point by giving Piggy a foil in the charismatic Jack, whose magnetic personality allows him to capture and wield power effectively, if not always wisely."

4. Develop and Organize Arguments

The reasons and examples that support your thesis will form the middle paragraphs of your essay. Since you can't really write your thesis statement until you know how you'll structure your argument, you'll probably end up working on steps 3 and 4 at the same time.

There's no single method of argumentation that will work in every context. One essay prompt might ask you to compare and contrast two characters, while another asks you to trace an image through a given work of literature. These questions require different kinds of answers and therefore different kinds of arguments. Below, we'll discuss three common kinds of essay prompts and some strategies for constructing a solid, well-argued case.

Types of Literary Essays

- **Compare and contrast**

  Compare and contrast the characters of Huck and Jim in The Adventures of Huckleberry Finn.

  Chances are you've written this kind of essay before. In an academic literary context, you'll organize your arguments the same way you would in any other class. You can either go *subject by subject* or *point by point*. In the former, you'll discuss one character first and then the second. In the latter, you'll choose several traits (attitude toward life, social status, images and metaphors associated with the character) and devote a paragraph to each. You may want to use a mix of these two approaches—for example, you may want to spend a paragraph a piece broadly sketching Huck's and Jim's personalities before transitioning into a paragraph or two that describes a few key points of comparison. This can be a highly effective strategy if you want to make a counterintuitive argument—that, despite seeming to be totally different, the two objects being compared are actually similar in a very important way (or vice versa). Remember that your essay should reveal something fresh or unexpected about the text, so think beyond the obvious parallels and differences.

- **Trace**

  Choose an image—for example, birds, knives, or eyes—and trace that image throughout Macbeth.

  Sounds pretty easy, right? All you need to do is read the play, underline every appearance of a knife in *Macbeth*, and then list them in your essay in the order they appear, right? Well, not exactly. Your teacher doesn't want a simple catalog of examples. He or she wants to see you make *connections* between those examples—that's the difference between summarizing and analyzing. In the *Macbeth* example above, think about the different contexts in which knives appear in the play and to what effect. In *Macbeth,* there are real knives and imagined knives; knives that kill and knives that simply threaten. Categorize and classify your examples to give them some order. Finally, always keep the overall effect in mind. After you choose and analyze your examples, you should come to some greater understanding about the work, as well as your chosen image, symbol, or phrase's role in developing the major themes and stylistic strategies of that work.

- **Debate**

  Is the society depicted in 1984 *good for its citizens?*

  In this kind of essay, you're being asked to debate a moral, ethical, or aesthetic issue regarding the work. You might be asked to judge a character or group of characters (*Is Caesar responsible for his own demise?*) or the work itself (*Is* JANE EYRE *a feminist novel?*). For this kind of essay, there are two important points to keep in mind. First, don't simply base your arguments on your personal feelings and reactions. Every literary essay expects you to read and analyze the work, so search for evidence in the text. What do characters in *1984* have to say about the government of Oceania? What images does Orwell use that might give you a hint about his attitude toward the government? As in any debate, you also need to make sure that you define all the necessary terms before you begin to argue your case. What does it mean to be a "good" society? What makes a novel "feminist"? You should define your terms right up front, in the first paragraph after your introduction.

  Second, remember that strong literary essays make contrary and surprising arguments. Try to think outside the box. In the *1984* example above, it seems like the obvious answer would be no, the totalitarian society depicted in Orwell's novel is *not* good for its citizens. But can you think of any arguments for the opposite side? Even if your final assertion is that the novel depicts a cruel, repressive, and therefore harmful society, acknowledging and responding to the counterargument will strengthen your overall case.

5. Write the Introduction

Your introduction sets up the entire essay. It's where you present your topic and articulate the particular issues and questions you'll be addressing. It's also where you, as the writer, introduce yourself to your readers. A persuasive literary essay immediately establishes its writer as a knowledgeable, authoritative figure.

An introduction can vary in length depending on the overall length of the essay, but in a traditional five-paragraph essay it should be no longer than one paragraph. However long it is, your introduction needs to:

- **Provide any necessary context.** Your introduction should situate the reader and let him or her know what to expect. What book are you discussing? Which characters? What topic will you be addressing?
- **Answer the "So what?" question.** Why is this topic important, and why is your particular position on the topic noteworthy? Ideally, your introduction should pique the reader's interest by suggesting how your argument is surprising or otherwise counterintuitive. Literary essays make unexpected connections and reveal less-than-obvious truths.
- **Present your thesis.** This usually happens at or very near the end of your introduction.
- **Indicate the shape of the essay to come.** Your reader should finish reading your introduction with a good sense of the scope of your essay as well as the path you'll take toward proving your thesis. You don't need to spell out every step, but you do need to suggest the organizational pattern you'll be using.

Your introduction should not:

- **Be vague.** Beware of the two killer words in literary analysis: *interesting* and *important.* Of course the work, question, or example is interesting and important—that's why you're writing about it!
- **Open with any grandiose assertions.** Many student readers think that beginning their essays with a flamboyant statement such as, "Since the dawn of time, writers have been fascinated with the topic of free will," makes them

sound important and commanding. You know what? It actually sounds pretty amateurish.

- **Wildly praise the work.** Another typical mistake student writers make is extolling the work or author. Your teacher doesn't need to be told that "Shakespeare is perhaps the greatest writer in the English language." You can mention a work's reputation in passing—by referring to *The Adventures of Huckleberry Finn* as "Mark Twain's enduring classic," for example—but don't make a point of bringing it up unless that reputation is key to your argument.
- **Go off-topic.** Keep your introduction streamlined and to the point. Don't feel the need to throw in all kinds of bells and whistles in order to impress your reader—just get to the point as quickly as you can, without skimping on any of the required steps.

---

6. Write the Body Paragraphs

Once you've written your introduction, you'll take the arguments you developed in step 4 and turn them into your body paragraphs. The organization of this middle section of your essay will largely be determined by the argumentative strategy you use, but no matter how you arrange your thoughts, your body paragraphs need to do the following:

- **Begin with a strong topic sentence.** Topic sentences are like signs on a highway: they tell the reader where they are and where they're going. A good topic sentence not only alerts readers to what issue will be discussed in the following paragraph but also gives them a sense of what argument will be made *about* that issue. "Rumor and gossip play an important role in *The Crucible*" isn't a strong topic sentence because it doesn't tell us very much. "The community's constant gossiping creates an environment that allows false accusations to flourish" is a much stronger topic sentence—it not only tells us *what* the paragraph will discuss (gossip) but *how* the paragraph will discuss the topic (by showing how gossip creates a set of conditions that leads to the play's climactic action).
- **Fully and completely develop a single thought.** Don't skip around in your paragraph or try to stuff in too much material. Body paragraphs are like bricks: each individual

one needs to be strong and sturdy or the entire structure will collapse. Make sure you have really proven your point before moving on to the next one.

- **Use transitions effectively.** Good literary essay writers know that each paragraph must be clearly and strongly linked to the material around it. Think of each paragraph as a response to the one that precedes it. Use transition words and phrases such as *however, similarly, on the contrary, therefore,* and *furthermore* to indicate what kind of response you're making.

---

7. Write the Conclusion

Just as you used the introduction to ground your readers in the topic before providing your thesis, you'll use the conclusion to quickly summarize the specifics learned thus far and then hint at the broader implications of your topic. A good conclusion will:

- **Do more than simply restate the thesis.** If your thesis argued that *The Catcher in the Rye* can be read as a Christian allegory, don't simply end your essay by saying, "And that is why *The Catcher in the Rye* can be read as a Christian allegory." If you've constructed your arguments well, this kind of statement will just be redundant.
- **Synthesize the arguments, not summarize them.** Similarly, don't repeat the details of your body paragraphs in your conclusion. The reader has already read your essay, and chances are it's not so long that they've forgotten all your points by now.
- **Revisit the "So what?" question.** In your introduction, you made a case for why your topic and position are important. You should close your essay with the same sort of gesture. What do your readers know now that they didn't know before? How will that knowledge help them better appreciate or understand the work overall?
- **Move from the specific to the general.** Your essay has most likely treated a very specific element of the work—a single character, a small set of images, or a particular passage. In your conclusion, try to show how this narrow discussion has wider implications for the work overall. If your essay on *To Kill a Mockingbird* focused on the character of Boo Radley, for example, you might want to include a bit in your

conclusion about how he fits into the novel's larger message about childhood, innocence, or family life.

- **Stay relevant.** Your conclusion should suggest new directions of thought, but it shouldn't be treated as an opportunity to pad your essay with all the extra, interesting ideas you came up with during your brainstorming sessions but couldn't fit into the essay proper. Don't attempt to stuff in unrelated queries or too many abstract thoughts.
- **Avoid making overblown closing statements.** A conclusion should open up your highly specific, focused discussion, but it should do so without drawing a sweeping lesson about life or human nature. Making such observations may be part of the point of reading, but it's almost always a mistake in essays, where these observations tend to sound overly dramatic or simply silly.

A+ Essay Checklist

Congratulations! If you've followed all the steps we've outlined above, you should have a solid literary essay to show for all your efforts. What if you've got your sights set on an A+? To write the kind of superlative essay that will be rewarded with a perfect grade, keep the following rubric in mind. These are the qualities that teachers expect to see in a truly A+ essay. How does yours stack up?

- ✓ Demonstrates a thorough understanding of the book
- ✓ Presents an original, compelling argument
- ✓ Thoughtfully analyzes the text's formal elements
- ✓ Uses appropriate and insightful examples
- ✓ Structures ideas in a logical and progressive order
- ✓ Demonstrates a mastery of sentence construction, transitions, grammar, spelling, and word choice

Suggested Essay Topics

1. *How does the suicidal impulse that both Romeo and Juliet exhibit relate to the overall theme of young love? Does Shakespeare seem to consider a self-destructive tendency inextricably connected with love, or is it a separate issue? Why do you think so?*

2. *Discuss the relationships between parents and children in* Romeo and Juliet. *How do Romeo and Juliet interact with their parents? Are they rebellious, in the modern sense? How do their parents feel about them?*

3. *Apart from clashing with Tybalt, what role does Mercutio play in the story? Is he merely a colorful supporting character and brilliant source of comic relief, or does he serve a more serious purpose?*

4. *How does Shakespeare treat death in* Romeo and Juliet? *Frame your answer in terms of legal, moral, familial, and personal issues. Bearing these issues in mind, compare the deaths of Romeo and Juliet, Romeo and Mercutio, and Mercutio and Tybalt.*

A+ Student Essay

In *Romeo and Juliet,* which is more powerful: fate or the characters' own actions?

In the opening Prologue of *Romeo and Juliet,* the Chorus refers to the title characters as "star-crossed lovers," an allusion to the belief that stars and planets have the power to control events on Earth. This line leads many readers to believe that Romeo and Juliet are inescapably destined to fall in love and equally destined to have that love destroyed. However, though Shakespeare's play raises the possibility that some impersonal, supernatural force shapes Romeo and Juliet's lives, by the end of the play it becomes clear that the characters bear more of the responsibility than Fortune does.

Though the Prologue offers the first and perhaps most famous example of celestial imagery in *Romeo and Juliet,* references to the stars, sun, moon, and heavens run throughout the play, and taken as a whole that imagery seems to express a different view of human responsibility. In Act I, scene iv, Romeo says that he fears "some consequence yet hanging in the stars" when he and his gang approach the Capulet's ball. In his next mention of stars, however, Romeo doesn't refer to their astrological power. Rather, he uses the image of stars to describe Juliet's otherworldly beauty. Most of the subsequent celestial images in the play follow in this vein, from Romeo's love-struck comparison of Juliet to the sun to Juliet's own wish to "cut [Romeo] out into little stars" when he dies. Throughout the play, these astral images are more often associated with the two lovers than with divine fate, emphasizing that, as the play's action escalates, we cannot simply place the blame for the tragedy on some impersonal external force.

It's true that Romeo and Juliet have some spectacularly bad luck. Tybalt picks a fatal fight with Romeo on the latter's wedding day, causing Capulet to move up the wedding with Paris. The crucial letter from Friar Lawrence goes missing due to an ill-timed outbreak of the plague. Romeo kills himself mere moments before Juliet wakes up. It's also true that the lovers aren't solely responsible for their difficult situation: Their friends, their families, and their society each played a role in creating the tragic circumstances. However, even if we allow that fate or some other divine force caused Romeo and Juliet to fall in love at first sight, thereby setting the action into motion, Shakespeare makes it clear that the characters' own decisions push that situation to its tragic conclusion. Either Romeo or Juliet, it is suggested, could have halted the headlong rush into destruction at any of several points.

Romeo's propensity for rash action gets him—and his beloved—in a lot of trouble. His impulsiveness has made him a romantic icon in our culture, but in the play it proves his undoing. From the very beginning, Shakespeare cautions us not to view Romeo's sudden fits of passion too idealistically—after all, Shakespeare makes a point to show that Romeo's love for Juliet merely displaced another, earlier infatuation. Through his hasty actions, Romeo arguably drives the play toward tragedy more aggressively than any other character. He climbs over Juliet's wall the night they meet and presses her to bind herself to him. He kills Tybalt in a blind rage. Then, thinking Juliet dead, he poisons himself. Romeo never thinks his actions through, and his lack of foresight makes him responsible for their dire consequences.

Though Juliet proves a strong-willed partner for Romeo, she bears less of the blame for their joint fate because she, at least, is wary of the speed at which they progress. In the balcony scene, she compares their love to lightning, which flares up suddenly but can just as quickly fade into darkness. Unlike Romeo, each of Juliet's fateful choices is a logical response to a situation. She agrees to marry him because she needs evidence that he is truly committed to her. She takes the potion not out of despair, but because she believes Friar Lawrence's plan will set things to rights. Though each of her choices ends up getting her and her lover deeper into trouble, those choices are at least the result of sober, careful reflection. Only when she sees her beloved dead does she succumb to his style of rashness, killing herself out of grief.

Romeo and Juliet concludes with a strong condemnation of the characters' actions. In the closing family portrait, the Capulets and the Montagues gather around the tomb to witness the consequences of their absurd conflict. Even if you don't believe that Romeo and Juliet could have saved themselves, you must admit that their families' blind hatred caused the situation, not the gods. As the Prince notes, even "[t]he sun for sorrow will not show his head" on that tragic day—even the heavens are pained at the human foolishness they see below.

Glossary of Literary Terms

ANTAGONIST
The entity that acts to frustrate the goals of the *protagonist*. The antagonist is usually another *character* but may also be a non-human force.

ANTIHERO / ANTIHEROINE
A *protagonist* who is not admirable or who challenges notions of what should be considered admirable.

CHARACTER
A person, animal, or any other thing with a personality that appears in a *narrative*.

CLIMAX
The moment of greatest intensity in a text or the major turning point in the *plot*.

CONFLICT
The central struggle that moves the *plot* forward. The conflict can be the *protagonist*'s struggle against fate, nature, society, or another person.

FIRST-PERSON POINT OF VIEW
A literary style in which the *narrator* tells the story from his or her own *point of view* and refers to himself or herself as "I." The narrator may be an active participant in the story or just an observer.

HERO / HEROINE
The principal *character* in a literary work or *narrative*.

IMAGERY
Language that brings to mind sense-impressions, representing things that can be seen, smelled, heard, tasted, or touched.

MOTIF
A recurring idea, structure, contrast, or device that develops or informs the major *themes* of a work of literature.

NARRATIVE
A story.

NARRATOR
The person (sometimes a *character*) who tells a story; the *voice* assumed by the writer. The narrator and the author of the work of literature are not the same person.

PLOT
The arrangement of the events in a story, including the sequence in which they are told, the relative emphasis they are given, and the causal connections between events.

POINT OF VIEW
The *perspective* that a *narrative* takes toward the events it describes.

PROTAGONIST
The main *character* around whom the story revolves.

SETTING
The location of a *narrative* in time and space. Setting creates mood or atmosphere.

SUBPLOT
A secondary *plot* that is of less importance to the overall story but may serve as a point of contrast or comParison to the main plot.

SYMBOL
An object, *character,* figure, or color that is used to represent an abstract idea or concept. Unlike an *emblem,* a symbol may have different meanings in different contexts.

SYNTAX
The way the words in a piece of writing are put together to form lines, phrases, or clauses; the basic structure of a piece of writing.

THEME
A fundamental and universal idea explored in a literary work.

TONE
The author's attitude toward the subject or *characters* of a story or poem or toward the reader.

VOICE
An author's individual way of using language to reflect his or her own personality and attitudes. An author communicates voice through *tone, diction,* and *syntax.*

A Note on Plagiarism

Plagiarism—presenting someone else's work as your own—rears its ugly head in many forms. Many students know that copying text without citing it is unacceptable. But some don't realize that even if you're not quoting directly, but instead are paraphrasing or summarizing, *it is plagiarism* unless you cite the source.

Here are the most common forms of plagiarism:

- Using an author's phrases, sentences, or paragraphs without citing the source
- Paraphrasing an author's ideas without citing the source
- Passing off another student's work as your own

How do you steer clear of plagiarism? You should *always* acknowledge all words and ideas that aren't your own by using quotation marks around verbatim text or citations like footnotes and endnotes to note another writer's ideas. For more information on how to give credit when credit is due, ask your teacher for guidance or visit www.sparknotes.com.

Review & Resources

Quiz

1. To which city does Romeo go after being exiled from Verona?

   A. Padua
   B. Rome
   C. Venice
   D. Mantua

2. Why is Romeo exiled?

   A. For killing Tybalt
   B. For marrying Juliet against her father's will
   C. For killing Mercutio
   D. For publicly admitting his atheism

3. Who performs Romeo and Juliet's marriage?

   A. Friar John
   B. Friar Lawrence
   C. Father Vincentio
   D. Mercutio

4. Who is the fairy that Mercutio says visits Romeo in dreams?

   A. Puck
   B. Queen Mab
   C. Beelzebub
   D. Jack o' the Clover

5. What does the Nurse advise Juliet to do after Romeo is exiled?

   A. Follow her husband to Mantua
   B. Wait for Romeo in Verona
   C. Act as if Romeo is dead and marry Paris
   D. Commit suicide

6. Where do Romeo and Juliet meet?

   A. At Capulet's feast
   B. At Friar Lawrence's cell
   C. At Montague's feast
   D. At the pier from which Malvolio is departing for Spain

7. Who kills Mercutio?

   A. Benvolio
   B. Sampson
   C. Romeo
   D. Tybalt

8. Which character first persuades Romeo to attend the feast?

   A. Mercutio
   B. Benvolio
   C. Lady Montague
   D. Juliet

9. What, at first, does Juliet claim that Romeo hears the morning after their wedding night?

   A. The owl
   B. The dove
   C. The nightingale
   D. The lark

10. To what does Romeo first compare Juliet during the balcony scene?

   A. The moon
   B. The stars
   C. A summer's day
   D. The morning sun

11. Who discovers Juliet after she takes Friar Lawrence's potion?

   A. Lady Capulet
   B. Capulet
   C. Paris
   D. The Nurse

12. Who proposes that a gold statue of Juliet be built in Verona?

A. Montague
B. Lady Capulet
C. Paris
D. Romeo

13. To which powerful figure is Paris related?

A. Capulet
B. Montague
C. Prince Escalus
D. King Vardamo

14. How and where does Romeo commit suicide?

A. With a dagger in the orchard
B. With a rope in the public square
C. With a sword in Juliet's bedchamber
D. With poison in Juliet's tomb

15. Who is the last person to see Juliet before she stabs herself dead?

A. Paris
B. Friar Lawrence
C. Tybalt
D. Romeo

16. Why is Friar John unable to deliver Friar Lawrence's message to Romeo in Mantua?

A. He is killed by a Capulet servant.
B. He is attacked by bandits on the road.
C. He is held inside a quarantined house, and is unable to leave.
D. Romeo is stopped in Padua and never makes it to Mantua.

17. Why does the Apothecary agree to sell Romeo poison?

    A. He is poor and needs the money.
    B. He can see that Romeo is passionate.
    C. He is afraid that Romeo will hurt him if he refuses.
    D. He is a friend of Friar Lawrence.

18. On what day do Romeo and Juliet meet?

    A. Saturday
    B. Tuesday
    C. Sunday
    D. Wednesday

19. With whom is Romeo madly in love for the first two scenes of the play?

    A. Himself
    B. Mercutio
    C. Juliet
    D. Rosaline

20. In what decade was Romeo and Juliet written?

    A. 1570s
    B. 1600s
    C. 1610s
    D. 1590s

21. Whom does Mercutio curse as he lies dying after a duel?

    A. The Montagues and Capulets
    B. Romeo
    C. Tybalt
    D. Romeo and Tybalt

22. In what area is Friar Lawrence an expert?

    A. Roman history
    B. Languages
    C. Plants and herbs
    D. Swordfighting

23. What term does the Chorus use to describe the lovers?

A. ill-fated
B. death-doom'd
C. demon-haunted
D. star-crossed

24. Why does Tybalt first challenge Romeo to a duel?

A. He is offended that Romeo loves his cousin.
B. He is offended that Romeo shows up at the Capulet ball.
C. He is offended that Romeo bites his thumb at him.
D. Tybalt does not challenge Romeo to a duel; he challenges Mercutio.

25. In what year did Shakespeare die?

A. 1610
B. 1594
C. 1601
D. 1616

ANSWER KEY

1: D; 2: A; 3: B; 4: B; 5: C; 6: A; 7: D; 8: B; 9: C; 10: D; 11: D; 12: A;
13: C; 14: D; 15: B; 16: C; 17: A; 18: C; 19: D; 20: D; 21: A; 22: C;
23: D; 24: B; 25: D

Suggestions for Further Reading

BLOOM, HAROLD. *Shakespeare: The Invention of the Human.* New York: Riverhead Books, 1999.

BLOOM, HAROLD, ed. *William Shakespeare's* ROMEO AND JULIET. New York: Chelsea House, 2000.

BRADBOOK, M. C. *Themes and Conventions of Elizabethan Tragedy,* 2nd edition. New York: Cambridge University Press, 1980.

DUSINBERRE, JULIET. *Shakespeare and the Nature of Women.* New York: Palgrave Macmillan, reprint edition 2003.

GREENBLATT, STEPHEN. "Introduction to *Romeo and Juliet.*" *The Norton Shakespeare.* New York: W. W. Norton and Company, 1997.

HALIO, JAY L., ed. *Shakespeare's* ROMEO AND JULIET: *Texts, Contexts and Interpretations.* Newark, NJ: University of Delaware Press, 1996.

SEWARD, JAMES H. *Tragic Vision in* ROMEO AND JULIET. Washington, D.C.: Consortium Press, 1973.

TANSELLE, G. THOMAS. "Time in *Romeo and Juliet,*" in *Shakespeare Quarterly,* v.15.4. Washington, D.C.: Folger Shakespeare Library, 1957.

VAN DOREN, MARK. *Shakespeare.* New York: Random House, reprint edition 2005.